Marriage
MATTERS
(LOVE, SEX & MONEY)

SADICK ARTHUR

Marriage Matters Love, Sex & Money

Unless otherwise indicated, scripture quotations are taken from the New King James Version of the Bible.

Sadick Arthur
International Central Gospel Church
P. O. Box 822
Ashburn, VA 20146
U.S.A.
Website: www.sadickarthur.org
Email: Sadick@centralgospelva.org

ISBN:

978-0-9676673-5-6

Printed in the USA by
Total Printing Systems
201 South Gregory Drive
Newton, IL 62448
1-800-465-5200

Contents

Dedication
Acknowledgment
Introduction

Chapter

Dedication

To my beautiful, esthetic, fine-looking, gorgeous, lovely, sweet, and stunning wife, Maame: your tenderness, patience, commitment, dedication, and prayers continue to make me into the ideal husband and father I am today. My heart continues to fond after you and my love for you continues to be renewed by the day. I am in love with you.

To my adored daughters, Merom and Melorra: may your marriages epitomize the model of a blissful marriage as laid down in the timeless principles of the Word of God.

To all couples desiring stable, steady and secure marriages. May the principles laid down in this book guide and provide you with the keys to successful marriages.

To the International Central Gospel Church for providing me in the early stages of my faith walk with the tools and teaching that has shaped my beliefs. The foundation and exposure I gained from the time-tested truths of the Bible at the Discipleship Training Program, Covenant Family meetings, and the weekly services have become my reference point to the stable Christian life I now enjoy.

Acknowledgments

I would like to thank Pastor and Mrs. Owusu for being reliable sources of inspiration to my ministry throughout the years. There are some who walk into the lives of others to make a mark. You have all made your mark and you continue to make a difference.

I would also like to thank Mr. and Mrs. Adonteng, Mr. and Mrs. Amoh, and Mr. and Mrs. Ofori Addo, for the vital supportive roles you play in my calling and ministry. Thank you Teiko Akufo for the editorial work.

Furthermore, I am grateful to Mr. and Mrs. Abbey, Mr. and Mrs. Quashie-Idun, Mr. and Mrs. Sarpong, Mr. and Mr. and Mrs. Asare, Mr. and Mrs. Sackey, Mr. and Mrs. Adusei Peasah, Mr. and Mrs. William Owusu, Mr. and Mrs. Richard Owusu, Mr. and Mrs. Yaw Arthur, Mr. and Mrs. Ofei, Mr. and Mrs. Boadi, Miss Beatrice Acquah, Mr. Claude Amaning, Mr. and Mrs. Asante, Ms. Regina Osei, Miss. Faustina Blay, Ms. Odilia Ocloo, and all the members of Fulfillment Temple. May your lives, marriages and homes be filled with beauty, bliss and blessings.

Introduction

If I were to ask you: marriage and driving, which of the two is more important, I believe you will say marriage. Yes, in contrast we all agree that driving cannot be compared to marriage in terms of its importance. Have you realized that although driving cannot in the least be compared to marriage, society somewhat assigns some level of importance to driving than to marriage? When you decide you want to start driving and you go to the Department of Motor Vehicles to apply for a driver's license, the department does not license you right away.

Before you are licensed to sit behind a car's steering wheel, you are given a written test to assess your level of knowledge on driving before you are given a permit to start learning how to drive. After you've been given a permit and have done a number of hours of practice on the road, you return to the Department of Motor Vehicles to be given a road test to ascertain your level of competence before you are issued a license and the privilege to drive.

Now, look at all the stages of preparation you have to go through before you're issued a driver's license. We all agree that marriage is far more important than driving. If people have to be prepared with written and road tests before they are licensed to sit behind the steering wheel of a car, why don't we apply the same level of preparation before permitting people to marry and before we put them behind the steering wheel of marriage so they don't wreck anyone's life?

I am of the opinion that people have to be adequately prepared before they marry. It is the absence of this preparation that accounts for the rather high level of divorce in our society today. This preparation can be in the form of spiritual guidance toward marriage or premarital counseling, where the potential couples are taught and tested to determine their preparedness for the holy and sacred institution.

Marriage does not create problems, yet problems inevitably show up in the institution. It is better for you to be prepared for the problems that inescapably show up than for the problems to show up and you are ill prepared. Without any prior preparation before entering into marriage, everything else comes as on-the-job training, which certainly will come with a price such as bumping into each other and learning whilst on the "job."

This book seeks to offer you tips to enjoying your marriage. If you never had the luxury of having any preparation prior to marriage, this book will make up for the inadequacy. If you did have an amount of counseling and ample preparation prior to marriage, this book will show you that there is more to know that you do not know yet, and that which you do not know is what I want to introduce to you here. Marriages have become bitter instead of better, and most are enduring instead of enjoying their marriages mainly because of ignorance. The wealth of knowledge encapsulated in this book, when imbibed without doubt will expel every iota of marital ignorance.

Chapter 1

God's Intention For Marriage

In this current era, marriage is no longer seen as a desirable institution. There are numerous individuals who reject marriage and would rather co inhabit and date someone they profess to love for years without committing to them in marriage. Traditional marriage, which is the union between a man and a woman has been under attack for decades now, and the opponents of the institution tend to be winning when we consider the latest wave of court decisions giving members of the homosexual community the same right as those in the heterosexual community.

Apart from the attacks on traditional marriage from the gay and lesbian communities notwithstanding, as well as attacks from the polygamy community, others are also defying marriage for the following reasons:

(I) A Type of Bondage

A number of people argue against marriage because they feel it is a type of bondage. They see marriage as a form of selling your freedom, and entangling yourself with another person for the duration of their lives. As a result of the anticipation of being restrained and constrained, to them, it's an absurd idea to marry.

(II) High Conflict Rate

There are others who also argue against marriage because they don't see the sense in entering an institution with a rather high conflict rate. Hence, they feel the high level of conflict that characterizes most marriages will make them miserable and unhappy when they commit to the same partner for life. With this mindset, such people feel marriage is an illogical idea for them.

(III) High Divorce Rate

The third reason why people argue against marriage is because of the high divorce rate. In the United States alone, it's believed that marriages have a seventy-five percent failure rate, and sadly, about fifty-five percent of children see their parents divorce before they leave home to start life on their own. Even Christians in mainline churches, who supposedly should know better are divorcing more rapidly than non-Christians, making it no longer attractive and appealing to enter the institution.

Despite what anyone thinks, God will never create or institute anything incongruous. James 1:17 tells us that, anything good and perfect comes from God. This indicates that God will never create anything bad. If He instituted marriage, which He did, marriage must then be a good thing.

The negative press given to marriage and high profile people who wrecked their marriages does not negate the fact that the institution is a good and perfect one. If you're not having a blissful marriage, it might be that you're unaware of the principles laid down in God's Word regarding the establishment.

Marriage Must Be Enjoyed

18 Here is what I have seen: It is good and fitting for one to eat and drink, and to enjoy the good of all his labor in which he toils under the sun all the days of his life which God gives him; for it is his heritage. 19 As for every man to whom God has given riches and wealth, and given him power to eat of it, to receive his heritage and rejoice in his labor – this is the gift of God.

Ecclesiastes 5:18-19

These two verses of scripture reveal three main points. First, it reveals that God wants us to enjoy our lives. Second, it shows that God wants us to be happy in life. Third, it tells us God takes pleasure in us enjoying life. God's intention for you is for you to enjoy life in its totality. In John 10:10, Jesus revealed that He incarnated so we would have life and have it abundantly. He wants you to enjoy your walk with Him, to enjoy your work life, secular life, including your marital life. In 1 Timothy 6:17, we learn that it is God, "who gives us richly all things to enjoy," including marriage. If God wants us to enjoy life and all things in life, He must want us to enjoy our marriages too.

Unfortunately, there are many married people who, rather than enjoying their marital lives, are enduring it. In Ecclesiastes 9:9, we are told, "live joyfully with the wife whom you love all the days of your life...for that is your portion in life." Do you see what God is saying here? God says it is your portion and your heritage in life to enjoy your spouse. This is referencing marital enjoyment.

Seek Knowledge

God did not intend for anything else to bring you delight and fulfillment in life like marriage does. The basic reason why most marriages are getting bitter instead of better, like I said in my introduction is because of ignorance. Ignorance is mankind's greatest enemy and it continues to fight us in every sphere of our lives including our marriages. What you don't know can kill you and what you don't know can easily destroy your marriage. If you come to embrace the truth that

God wants you to enjoy your marriage, you will work hard to make your marriage to work.

It's almost impossible to write a book of this caliber and not emphasize the importance of knowledge as a basis for marital success. Ignorance will destroy your marriage, and you fight ignorance with information. This book seeks to do just that: to place the necessary information you need for a blissful marriage at your fingertips.

The prophet Hosea writes that, "My people are destroyed for lack of knowledge..." (Hosea 4:6). Your marriage can be destroyed when you lack knowledge. If you are unmarried, you must make sure you submit to some spiritual guidance prior to marriage, and after you're married, you must ensure that you keep learning and studying the timeless biblical principles for marriage as is laid down in the Scriptures.

The Essentials of Marriage

Before we proceed further, I would like to define marriage from a biblical and godly standpoint and would use the keywords in the definition to emphasize God's intention for marriage. *By definition, marriage is supposed to be a steady and sexually exclusive relationship of sentimental care between straight people.* This is what traditional marriage is, and it's God's intention for the institution.

Hence, traditional marriage is a steady *(as long as you both shall live)* and sexually exclusive relationship *(forsaking all others; holding each other in the highest esteem above all others)* of sentimental care *(love, cherish and honor)* between straight people *(to be your wedded husband, to be your wedded wife).*

Present in this definition, are four essentials of marriage, which are:

1. A steady relationship

2. A sexually exclusive relationship

3. A sentimental relationship

4. A straight relationship

Chapter 2

A Steady Relationship

Marriage is a steady and sexually exclusive relationship of sentimental care between straight people.

By a steady relationship, I mean marriage ought to be a stable, permanent relationship. How can marriage be kept permanent in a society, which is becoming more and more anti-marriage? To answer this question, we need to go back to the Word of God to determine what God, the creator and institutor of marriage had in mind.

> [14] *...the LORD has been witness between you and the wife of your youth...she is your companion and your wife by covenant ...let none deal treacherously with the wife of his youth.* [16] *"For the LORD God of Israel says that He hates divorce.*
>
> *Malachi 2:14 and 16*

The one who instituted marriage is God. It is He who joined the first couple on earth together, and that was when He officiated the marriage ceremony of Adam and Eve in the Garden of Eden. He then said in Genesis 2:24, "therefore a man shall leave his father and mother and be joined to his wife, and they shall become one flesh." So you see that the one who instituted and oversaw the union of the first man and the woman is God, reemphasizing Him being the originator of marriage. Furthermore, it takes the originator to give the guidelines, rules and principles governing marriage.

God instituted marriage with the intention of it being a steady, stable and permanent love relationship, and because He intended for it to be steady and permanent, He mentioned that the relationship that exists between a husband and wife is akin to a covenant relationship.

Covenant Marriage

Marriage is a type of covenant, and the Scriptures tell us there are different kinds of covenants. However, the most potent and highest of all covenants is blood covenant. Blood covenants are not made to be broken; they are for life, and from what we read in Malachi 2:14, we learn that a man's wife is his companion by covenant, making marriage a type of covenant relationship. *If blood covenants are for life and marriage is a type of blood covenant, then marriage must of necessity be for life.* This explains why in our marriage vows, we make a commitment such as "till death do us part." The only thing that should separate a husband and wife should be death. Let's recap this:

- Marriage is a covenant relationship

- Marriage is a type of blood covenant

- Blood covenant is the highest form of covenant

- Blood covenant is not to be broken

- The only thing with the right to break blood covenant is death

I would like to reiterate that marriage is a type of blood covenant, which is not supposed to be broken. It is for life, and forever. When a man and a woman marry, they enter into covenant, and when you read Genesis 1:26, you find that God created mankind in His image and likeness, which means that mankind was made to function like God. In Psalm 89:34, the Bible again tells us that, God does not break covenants. Since we were originally created in God's image to function like Him, and since He doesn't break covenants, we also cannot break our marriage covenants.

Consequently, when you enter into marriage, it is for life. There is no getting out. Even if you are not happy, you remain steadfast and trust God to work it to work for you. Marriage is not a contract but a covenant relationship. Covenants are not like contracts. Contracts are easily broken whereas marriage is not meant to be broken. God hates it when the marriage covenant is broken.

Divorce Is Not An Option

As marriage is supposed to be a steady and a permanent covenant relationship, divorce and separation are not options. Marriage is not like going shopping for shoes, where you try it on, and when it's not comfortable, you dump it and try a different pair. In Malachi 2:16, the Bible tells us that, God "hates divorce." Whatever God hates, you should also hate. Even if you are having problems in your marriage, the solution is not divorce. *Divorce never solves marital problems, it rather compounds personal problems, and the impact of divorce is more devastating when there are children involved.*

Statistically, it's been proven over and over that children who grow without the benefits of a traditional family (that is, biological mother and father) have a 65% rate of becoming a burden on society by either committing a crime, being emotionally troubled, being mentally unstable, having out-of-wedlock children, being less educated, and unhealthy as compared to children whose parents lived together as husband and wife. For the sake of our children, you must fight for our marriages.

One should never consider divorce, as it is a way of turning your back at the Word of God. Divorce is a negative decision for you and for your children. Stay in there and trust God to make it work.

Due to the fact that divorce is not an option and because you don't want to be miserable in your marriage, you must reprogram yourself and renew your mind to enjoy your marriage and make it sizzle. Loosen up, forgive your spouse if there are any offenses, love your spouse, enjoy your spouse and have a great marriage.

Marriage Matters

Chapter 3

A Sexually Exclusive Relationship

Marriage is a steady and sexually exclusive relationship of sentimental care between straight people.

When a couple marries, they promise to hold each other in the highest esteem and to forsake all others and to be faithful to each other sexually. During the exchange of vows at a marriage ceremony, you hear the groom make a vow before God, the minister, witnesses, and to the bride "to hold her in the highest esteem above all women," and the bride does the same.

To vow to hold someone in the highest esteem for the rest of your life is what marriage is, a sexually exclusive relationship. Every other person is sexually excluded from the union.

Faithfulness in a marriage is so fundamental to the marriage agreement that when the vow is broken, most marriages go into a freefall. Infidelity ranks as one of the most painful experiences of a betrayed spouse's life. Anyone who knew at the time of their wedding that their spouse would eventually have an affair most definitely would refuse to marry that person. Adultery is a sin, and according to Galatians 5:18, it is the work of the flesh, and those who do this will not inherit the kingdom of God.

Infidelity usually starts with flirtations. It starts as a wrongful emotional desire for someone you're not married to, and when this desire is not put in check, it evolves into deception, where you convince yourself intellectually that there is nothing wrong with betraying your spouse's trust. After you've been trapped with deception, the flirtation develops to disobedience. Disobedience is the will to act, and that is when you actually commit the affair.

Apart from your spouse don't give anyone the chance to meet your intimate emotional needs. Your craving for intimacy, more so sexual intimacy must exclusively be satisfied by your spouse.

Never put yourself in a vulnerable position and by all means avoid being alone in a secluded place with someone you're not married to. Infidelity occurs when there is the lack of discipline; there is no fear of God, and there is the withholding of sex from the other person, which I will delve into later.

It is inherently wrong as a married person to have a close relationship, more so an intimate one with someone you're not married to, and there is everything inherently wrong with an unmarried fellow who engages a married person sexually. This is not just being an adulterous pervert and being unfaithful to your spouse but you're committing an iniquity and sowing a bad seed, which you could reap its consequences later.

Galatians 6:7 says "do not be deceived, God is not mocked; for whatever a man sows, that he will also reap." Whatever, seed you sow, the Bible says you will reap and God wasn't joking when He said that! Every action of yours has a corresponding consequence, and serious-minded people act, considering the impact of their actions on their families. Therefore, be careful of the kind of seed you sow. When children act they do not consider the impact of their actions on themselves and on others. Marriage is not for children but for the matured, hence you must be mindful of the impact of your actions.

David sowed the seed of adultery with Bathsheba. Little did he know that his actions would reap tragic consequences. His actions led to the death of the child that was born from the affair, his children became sexually perverted, rape and incest became the norm in his family as a result of the seed of adultery he sown and a poor decision he made. Once again, never put yourself in a vulnerable position to commit an adulterous act. It's sinful against God, your spouse and your children.

Honoring The Marriage Vow

There are many who go to the altar to marry and to exchange vows: firstly, to each other, secondly, before God, thirdly before the minister, and lastly before their families and friends, but sadly end up not taking their vows seriously.

It's believed that one out of every two couples dishonor their marriage vow, and the reason this happens is because they do not see their vows as sacred and holy. Anything holy, you must remember is accursed, and anything accursed has the capability to bring a curse. If anything holy is accursed, then, when you make that which is holy, unholy, it has the capability to bring a curse on you. The marriage vow is holy, and when you dishonor it, you make it unholy, which can bring you under a curse.

> *When you tell God you'll do something, do it — now.*
> *God takes no pleasure in foolish gabble. Vow it, then do*
> *it. Far better not to vow in the first place than to vow*
> *and not pay up.*

> *Ecclesiastes 5:4-5 (TM)*

From these two verses of Scripture, you realize that God calls those who break their vows, fools, and He also reveals that He does not take pleasure in vow-breakers. If God does not take pleasure in vow-breakers, it means that vow-breakers will without fail incur His displeasure. With regards to marriage, God says: "it is better for you not to say your marriage vow than to make the commitment and then not honor it."

Chapter 4

A Sentimental Relationship

Marriage is a steady and sexually exclusive relationship of sentimental care between straight people.

he third key phrase from the definition of marriage is that it is a sentimentally caring relationship. Marriage is a special caring relationship, and that is why in the exchange of vows, both the bride and the groom vow and makes commitment to love, honor and cherish each other for the rest of their lives. The idea of loving, honoring and cherishing each other for life is what makes marriage a special, sentimentally caring relationship.

One of the primary reasons why a man and a woman

should decide to marry is because they want to share things in common. After they have exchanged vows, they are to continue sharing things in common and caring for each other. With this sentimental care, whatever affects your spouse should affect you. Whatever matters to your spouse must matter to you. You must take it upon yourself to express special, sentimental care to your spouse at all times. Simply, let them know that you care. Husbands: send her flowers. Call each other several times in a day. Send each other love notes. Texting and emailing each other to express your love and passion for each other should be the norm.

Buy each other gifts not only on special occasions but also in the mundane and ordinary moments of your journey of love. Cultivate the habit of bringing home a gift to your spouse. When you hold a gift in your hand intended for your spouse, the message it communicates to him or her is, my honey was thinking of me. If craving for special, sentimental care is your spouse's romance language, you will go a long way in making his or her day, and positively affecting his or her mood for the day, which will trickle down to the bedroom.

Through my years of being a pastor, coaching and counseling couples, I have realized a common pattern of complains from women with regards to their husbands, and it is the phrase: "he doesn't care." Special, sentimental care matters especially to women. Most women feel special and loved when you show them that you care, and you can show that you care by doing some of the things you consider trivial, insignificant, and inconsequential.

Ways To Show Your Wife You Care

When was the last time you did something sweet for the woman you love? Let me show you a lighthearted list of easy, painless ways to let your wife know that you appreciate her:

(I) Surprise Her With Gifts

Buy your wife a gift you are certain she would love and appreciate at a period of time she least expects it. Nothing communicates special, sentimental care to a wife as being frequently surprised with gifts.

(II) Send A Message

Have the habit of sending your wife a message. Send her emails and text messages flirting with her, complimenting her, affirming her, and thanking her for the way she makes you feel good. Have flowers delivered to her whilst she is at work and even at home. It sends a strong message that she is being thought of.

(III) Store Her Picture In Your Wallet

Women feel special, cared for and preferred above all other women when you keep their photo in your wallet. Everyone likes to feel extraordinary, cared for and loved.

(IV) Sanitize Something

Cleaning anything and anywhere in the house will do. If you think everything around the house is already spotless, at least, be thankful you have such an efficient wife, and go clean out her car. I know you are probably thinking that you don't want her to get used to this help, and that is why you are terrified of doing it even once. Realize this, if she is an overworked wife and mother, she will be thrilled.

(V) Smarten Up The House

Find anything that is broken or not working and fix it. Don't wait to be told to replace a dead bulb. Just do it! If you are oblivious to what needs fixing, just ask her. She probably would have an already prepared list. My wife always writes the date air filters are changed, and to help smarten up the house, I schedule the task on my smart phone to remind me to replace the filters with new ones every three months, without being told.

(VI) See To The Grocery Shopping

Ask your wife for a grocery list and go pick her the items. Tell her, you want her to take a break whilst you run the errands for the home. While you are at the grocery, go the extra mile and buy her something that is not on the list, like her favorite candy or other treat. Just a word of caution: do not buy her favorite chocolate cake if she is on a diet, unless you're prepared to not say a thing about her weight.

(VII) Subsidize Her Sleep

On a Saturday morning, allow her to wake up late. Even if you can only keep the kids quiet for an hour so she can have an extended sleep, do it! That will have a great impact on her morning. Bring her some coffee or tea in bed when she wakes up. Feed the kids while you are at it to minimize the amount of work she has to do when she arises from bed!

(VIII) Select Weekly Dinner

Take her and the children out at least once every other week. On other weeknights, pick up dinner on your way home from work so she doesn't have to cook or so she doesn't feel guilty for making you warm something up yourself. When picking up dinner, be sensitive enough to pick up her favorite food, instead of yours.

(IX) Spend Time With The Children

Tell her to go take a couple of hours for herself, probably to visit the salon for a hairdo, a manicure, a pedicure, or something while you happily play with the kids. The fact that you offered, and she doesn't have to beg or look at a sour face as she walks out the door will do wonders for your marriage.

(X) Sincere Nag-Free Day

Everyone always talks of nagging wives, but what about nagging husbands? Take a good, long look at yourself, just to be sure. Do you nag her? Let it go, just this once and allow her time without trivial complaints and faultfinding.

Ways To Show Your Husband You Care

Men also want to feel special and cared for, and below are some of the ways a wife could show her husband she cares:

(I) Superlative Fan

Let him know you are his biggest, superlative fan. Tell him how great he is, how much you appreciate the little things he does to help you and how much he's loved. I am not suggesting you lie but if you are not his biggest fan and you remain married to him, you must have a change of heart and start celebrating him. Being his biggest fan will make him feel you care.

(II) Speak Highly Of Him

Always speak highly of him to others. Don't call up your best friend, your mom or dad to tell him or her about his latest gaffe or unintelligent mistake. There are four A's in marriage: Affection, Appreciation, Approval and Acceptance. Accept him for who he is and focus on his strengths rather than his weaknesses.

(III) Submit To Him

God made men to function on respect and when he feels disrespected he will malfunction at home. Ephesians 5:33

instruct wives to respect and be submissive to their husbands. The word respect denotes to hold in high esteem. Apart from being his fan and speaking highly of him, you must also hold him in high esteem. Sarah understood this principle of respecting and submitting to a husband the Bible says in 1 Peter 3:5-6 that, "for this is how the holy women who hoped in God also adorned themselves, being submissive to their husbands, as Sarah obeyed Abraham, calling him lord, whose daughters you are..."

Never cut your man down. It may be tempting to tell him exactly what you think of him during an argument, but hold your tongue. Deep down, somewhere, you love this man. Tearing him apart and shredding him to bits and pieces will only make the situation worse.

(IV) Speedily Apologize

Do not underestimate the power of apology. Be quick to apologize for snapping at him when you are tired and cranky. This will make him feel you care. More so, apology is like medicine. It cures the infirmity of an argument.

(V) Sincerely Listen To What He Has To Say

Listen to your man when he speaks. Both men and women are interested in their spouses listening to them when they speak as opposed to hearing them. Listening and hearing are two separate things. Hearing is just sound waves hitting your eardrum, but listening involves perceiving the sound waves that hit your eardrum. Even when you don't understand nor care to be enlightened about what he is saying, still listen!

(VI) Stare At Him With Gratitude

Appreciate who he is and don't try to change him. You will be frustrated when you try to change him and disappointed when you try to make your marriage look like other people's marriage. You knew who he was before you married him, and even if you feel he's changed after marriage, the potential was there before you said, "I do."

Trying to make him into something different is a waste of your time because it will not work, and it's also just annoying. He was flawless in your eyes when you first met. Is he really not good enough now? I know, you have grown, changed, evolved and expanded. Allow him to be him. Accept him for who he is and appreciate him for the little things he does to make you happy.

(VII) Stimulate His Hobbies

Encourage his hobbies even if you aren't fond of them. Don't stop him from enjoying his hobbies because you don't like it. Always remember he is your husband, not your child. Men crave for recreational companionship. Becoming interested in his recreational activities communicates to him that you care. Take pleasure watching his favorite sport with him.

(VIII) Spur His Team

Don't tease or make fun of his team even if they always lose. It is likely that your husband has been programmed since birth to be a fan of a particular sports team. To tease him when his favorite team loses will anger him and communicate insensitivity and lack of care to him.

(IX) Set Up His Meals

There is a saying that the way to a man's heart is through his stomach. Although that is not always the case, it helps you to know that you can gain access to his heart by ensuring he is not starved and that there is always food on the table for him to enjoy. Give out your best when you cook, and with so many good cookbooks and variety of free recipes on the World Wide Web, you can easily astound him with what you dish out to him. With so much free information at our disposal, it's unacceptable for a lady to fail in the kitchen.

(X) Sweet Wife

Every husband will be thankful for a pleasant wife. Cause your husband no pain and give him no headache. Let him enjoy being around you, being at home, and constantly ensure he sees you as that pleasant, sweet person he saw prior to marriage. Also, a man feels cared for when his sexual needs are always met. A man feels cared for when his intimate needs are always met.

Chapter 5

A Straight Relationship

Marriage is a steady and sexually exclusive relationship of
sentimental care between straight people.

The last key phrase in our definition of marriage is that marriage is a straight relationship. By straight, I mean God intended marriage to be between heterosexual couples. Marriage was instituted by God to be between a man and a woman.

When God said it was not good for man to be alone and that He would make him a suitable mate, the suitable mate He made was a woman called Eve. This shows that God's original intent for marriage is that it should be a one man, one-woman relationship, and it is this one man, one-woman relationship that I call a straight relationship.

41

In a marriage vow, the groom promises to take the bride to be his wedded wife, and the bride also promises to take the groom to be her wedded husband. This means that marriage is between a husband and a wife. Any other lifestyle or sexual preference does not fall in this category. So the courts are wrong trying to define marriage to include gays and lesbians. God who instituted marriage says it's for straight people. Marriage is sacred and a holy institution and it should be kept in its sanctity.

Chapter 6

The Power Of Love

There are three things that affect marriage more than any other, and they are love, sex and money. I am going to take the next several chapters to discuss them. Let's begin with love, looking at it from a biblical perspective and what role it plays in a marriage.

Biblical Perspective of Love

(1) Love is the foundation of every successful marriage

Marriage works better and is beautiful and blissful when husband and wife are in love with each other. So in Ephesians 5:23, the Bible tells husbands, "love your wives, just as Christ also loved the church and gave Himself for her." And in Titus 2:4, the Bible again says, "…Admonish the young women to love their husbands…"

These two verses of scripture show that a husband must love his wife just as a wife must also love her husband. *The foundation of every successful marriage is love. Remember: marriage is better, beautiful and blissful when a husband and wife love each other dearly.*

(2) Love is the force that binds marriage together

Notice that if it took love to join a man and woman together in marriage, it will take love to maintain and sustain their marriage. When love waxes cold and dissipates in a marriage, the marriage suffers and eventually breaks apart. The Bible says in 1 Corinthians 13:8, that everything else will fail, but "love never fails." If you want to succeed in marriage, ensure your professed love is genuine and unshakable.

Love is what makes a husband and a wife stay committed to their marriage and to each other for the rest of their lives. There are three C's to a steady marriage; Commitment, Communication and Conflict resolution. Apart from love being the force that binds a couple together and make them remain committed to their marriage, love is also that which makes a couple communicate effectively and seek solution from the Word of God to resolve the conflicts that arise in their marriage.

(3) Love is the forgiving force in marriage

Offences in a marriage are inevitable. *When two people with different upbringing and varied backgrounds come together in marriage under the same roof, the tendency of conflict and offense is high and inevitable. Love is the force that makes you look past the offense of your lover.*

People divorce because they do not understand this biblical perspective of love. When you are truly in love with each other, love makes you bear no grudge and offence. It rather makes you excuse the offences of your lover. In 1 Corinthians 13:4-5, the Bible tells us that, love bears all things and keeps no record of wrong. 1 Peter 4:8 also instructs us to, "have fervent love for one another, for love covers a multitude of sins."

If you want to marry and not divorce, ensure that the person you want to marry truly loves you and that you also truly love the person. If you truly do, your love for each other will be the force that carries you through your moments of turbulence, misunderstandings, hurts and pain. Marriages remain blissful in the face of all odds and obstacles because of love. That is how powerful love is! Every married couple must guard against their love for each other growing cold. Solomon wrote of his love relationship with the Shulamite that; challenges, offences, conflicts, misunderstandings, and problems cannot be able to quench the love between them.

This is how he said it:

Many waters cannot quench love,
Nor can the floods drown it...

Song of Solomon 8:7

<u>Kinds of Love</u>

Although the usage of the word "love' is limited in the English language, the Greek language uses different terminologies to describe it, but I want to focus on five of the terminologies and they are:

- Epithumia: sexual love or lust

- Eros: erotic or romantic love

- Philostorgos: brotherly love or love for a brother or sister

- Phileo: friendly love or love for friends

- Agape: divine love

One major reason why you should marry is because you have found someone you want to express your personal love to. This personal love is a combination of epithumia, eros, philostorgos and phileo. However, another major reason why you should marry is because you also want to express agape to that person. Agape is not earthly like the others. Agape is God's love. Hence, because God has shown you love, you also want to take that level of love and express it to someone you personally love. Agape is unconditional love.

Agape is allowing God to love through you even when you don't want to love. Even when we did not deserve God's love, He still loved us.

But God demonstrates His own love toward us, in that while we were still sinners, Christ died for us.

Romans 5:8

So when you are offended by your spouse and angry at him or her, and do not want to show him or her love, agape is that which compels you to continue showing and demonstrating love. Divorce in marriage usually takes place when a party is offended and hurt, and the offense is not forgiven, leading to bitterness and resentment. Because the love of such people is not agape, they give up on their marriage. Remember; agape loves even when it is offended and hurt.

In a marriage, love requires that you remain forgiving, friendly and romantic. The secret to keeping love alive in a marriage is realizing that every one has a unique romance language that they crave for. I want to use the next chapter to discuss that with you.

Marriage Matters

Chapter 7

The Importance Of Romance In A Marriage

My assignment in this chapter is to show you from the Word of God, what romance is, how to be romantic, how to identify what your spouse considers romantic, and how to communicate his or her romance language. Failure to speak your spouse's romance language means you're prepared to quench the fire of love and eventually wreck your marriage.

Romance is not just important but very essential in marriage. *Romance is the engine that keeps the fire of love and the vehicle of marriage running strong.* Simply, romance makes marriage interesting. Without it, every marriage will move into a free fall. Another common complain I hear from wives is "my husband is not romantic, or my husband doesn't care," and the common carps I hear from husbands is "my wife doesn't understand me."

One day, whilst helping a couple resolve a conflict, I asked the woman, why do you say he is not romantic? She responded, "he doesn't tell me he loves me. He only says it when he is making love to me." I asked the husband why is that? He responded, "but she knows I love her! Do I have to say it all the time before she knows I love her?" This showed me that there are people who could be married for years and still don't know what their spouses consider romantic.

How To Be Romantic

Romance is expressed in so many ways but primarily in the following:

(1) Romance Is Expressed With Your Tongue

Every man and woman wants love to be expressed to them in a particular way, and it is the duty and responsibility of both husbands and wives to find out what their spouse's romance language is and communicate that to them on a regular basis. *A romance language is a verbal and non-verbal communication that when expressed at the right time with the right tone and motive easily titillates, stimulates and turns your spouse on.*

If you are married or have found someone you plan to marry, you need to carefully find out what his or her romance language is and consciously express it to him or her.

For some people their romance language is you expressing love to them with your tongue. *Expressing romance with your tongue means using your tongue to speak the right words.* For this person, the way to his or her heart is through his or her ears. This person wants you to look deeply into his or her eyes and say some nice words to his or her hearing. By words, I also mean words that affirm. How you speak with and talk to the person you profess to love is vital. Romantic love requires your words to your lover to be gracious and kind.

Your words to the person must be positive and constructive rather than negative, judgmental and condemning. If a person likes for you to express love to them with your tongue, and you use the same words they want to hear from your lips, not to affirm them but to condemn, criticize and insult them, they would feel deprived of love, will conclude that you are unromantic, and will malfunction and give you headaches at home.

God wants our words to be fitly spoken and carefully chosen. Let's examine the following:

> *A word fitly spoken is like apples of gold in settings of silver.*

> *Proverbs 25:11*

In making marital decisions, ensure the person you're planning on marrying and committing to share the rest of your life with has the ability to articulate his or her thoughts and feelings without putting you down. And if you are already married you must cultivate the art and ability of speaking graciously to your spouse. This is how God wants you to speak:

Let no corrupt word proceed out of your mouth, but what is good for necessary edification, that it may impart grace to the hearers.

Ephesians 4:29

One of Shulamite's primary romance languages was receiving sweet expressions. All through the book of Song of Solomon, you repeatedly hear Solomon using his tongue to affirm his lady, and the Shulamite herself affirmed this when she said:

O my dove...let me hear your voice; for your voice is sweet.

Song of Solomon 2:14

In other words, the Shulamite is telling her husband that the words his tongue utters is pleasant and sweet to her ears. For this woman, the best frequency her husband can use to get to her heart and to make her feel good about herself is expressing pleasant and sweet words to her. This scripture indicates that the way to this woman's heart is through her ears. As a husband, if you would learn to use words that are pleasant and sweet, your wife will always grant you access to her heart.

(2) Romance Is Expressed With Your Time

The three most valuable assets a person possesses are their time, their treasures, and their talents. True love makes you share these valuables without reservation.

You must enjoy spending time with your significant other than with your friends and on the job. By spending time I do not mean whiling away time but spending quality time to have quality conversation and quality fun activities.

What worthwhile time does is it brings the man and the woman together so they can bond more. This is what marriage is about: being together and bonding. For some people, their romance language is spending valuable time with their lover, and it is essential that you express love in this regard. They feel you are being romantic when you enjoy being around them. You must enjoy being in each other's arms whilst you chat, whilst you watch television and so forth.

In some homes, when a husband and his wife are watching television, one person sits here and the other sits there - they don't sit together. Meanwhile, they actually have a loveseat in their living room staring at them. The loveseat is not for decoration rather it's for you and your wife having quality time in it. Enjoy going to movies together. Enjoy taking a walk, working out, having a night out together.

In Song of Solomon 7:11, you notice the romantic language of precious, quality time being expressed when the Shulamite said:

> *Come, my beloved,*
> *Let us go forth to the fields;*
> *Let us lodge in the villages*
>
> *Song of Solomon 7:11*

You can deduce from the verse that she was craving for a good time, considering her words, "let us go forth." This precious time involved lodging "in the village." This is symbolic of taking a vacation or getting away on a weekend or a holiday just to have a good and a superb time. God wants husbands and wives to have terrific times together and this must be frequent and often. Let's examine what His Word says of the subject:

> *As a loving deer and a graceful doe, let her breasts*
> *satisfy you at all times; and always be enraptured with*
> *her love.*
>
> *Proverbs 5:19*

The emphasis is on the phrase, "at all times." This scripture is instructing men to spend lots of valuable times with their wives. If this is your spouse's romance language, you will do your marriage a big favor if you non-verbally communicate to him or her in this manner.

(3) Romance Is Expressed With Your Treasures

For others, the romance language they understand best is when you show them that you care about them. Some men and women feel you are romantic when they feel you care. You will know if a person cares about you if what affects you affect him or her. If you have a habit of giving your lover gifts, spending your treasures on him or her, remembering his or her birthday, anniversaries, and events that matter to him or her, and you make him or her know such events matter to you also, you will be using non-verbal language to communicate loads of love.

Don't buy your spouse a gift only on special occasions. In the ordinary days of your journey of love, habitually surprise each other with gifts, love notes, flowers, text messages, emails, and phone calls in which you express how much you care and love him or her. When was the last time you wrote a love note? Do you keep a picture of your husband or your wife in your wallet or purse?

Carrying his or her picture in your wallet or purse makes him or her feel you deeply love and care. I am proposing that from this moment, if you do not have your spouse's picture in your wallet or purse, find one and trim it and keep it on you. It tells your spouse you are madly in love with him or her.

True romantic love is expressed by expending your treasures. People don't care how much you profess to love them until they know you care about them. Caring is not expressed just in words but in deeds. Let's take a look at an example of a man who showed his wife romance with care.

> *Now it came to pass, when he had been there a long time, that Abimelech king of the Philistines looked through a window, and saw, and there was Isaac, <u>showing endearment</u> to Rebekah his wife.*

> *Genesis 26:8*

The word endearment as used in the above passage means affection, caring and caressing. As an Old Testament character, Isaac knew his wife's romance language and he communicated that to her. How much more you, a post New Testament character? You should know better and should show more endearment to your spouse.

(4) Romance Is Expressed With Your Talents

God has placed gifts, talents, strengths, and natural abilities in each and every one of us. He placed these talents in you even before you were born. In Jeremiah 1:5, He told Jeremiah; before I formed you in the womb I knew you, before you were born I sanctified you and appointed you a prophet to the nations. Over here, God is telling Jeremiah that He knew him and placed gifts and abilities in him before he was formed in his mother's womb.

Similarly, God has placed talents in you! Each one of us has been wired with something special. According to 1 Corinthians 7:7, "each one has his own gift from God, one in this manner and another in that." The emphasis is the word "own." You have your own unique, individual, distinctive, special gift and talent from God. It is your responsibility to find out what that gift is and maximize it. Failure to locate and cultivate your unique gift makes life meaningless.

There are people who feel you're romantic when you use your talents to pursue your destiny. For this person, fulfilling your life's purpose and making a difference communicates love to them. For this wife, seeing her husband climb the ladder of success and being able to share in his success is love. This is a nonverbal romance language and that is why all of us have to find out what our unique gifts are and commit to maximize them.

There is something that you enjoy doing. There is something you are effective at. There is something you are enthusiastic about. Find that thing and develop and deploy it to benefit humanity. You will feel fulfilled and will be communicating love to your spouse just by finding out what your unique gifts and talents are.

(5) Romance Is Expressed With Your Thinking

A husband should not be intimidated because his wife is smart and neither should a wife. Notwithstanding, there are some people who consider their spouse's intelligence and brilliance as being romantic. For this person, your ability to appeal to their mind sends a message of you being romantic.

Demonstrating your wealth of wisdom, grace and understanding of the issues of life turns their hearts toward you. If that's your spouse's romance language, you must read more, add value to yourself, increase your knowledge base, be in tune with the times, and be abreast with current affairs. This is because listening to you talk and display your wealth of knowledge is what appeals to their cerebral and it's what makes their heart fond more and more after you.

(6) Romance Is Expressed With Teamwork

Furthermore, there are others who feel you're being romantic when you express willingness to work with them as a team. Seeing your spouse as a partner and a teammate sends the message of a loving and caring husband or wife. There is nowhere in the Scriptures where women for instance are referred to as inferior. That said every husband owes it to God and to his wife to treat her as a teammate, a friend, a colleague and a coequal - for some women that is being sensitive and romantic.

Consulting your spouse before you make decisions affecting the home and soliciting his or her input before you make important decisions will make a big difference in determining the mood in your home.

If this is your husband's romance language and you deprive him of it, he will feel disrespected and label you a defiant wife. If that is your wife's romance language, denying her of it, will make her feel unwanted, unappreciated and treated as though she were subservient. This could hurt her self-esteem and consequently affect the marriage adversely.

(7) Romance Is Expressed With Your Touch

For other people true romantic love is expressed to them when you touch them. They feel you are romantic when you enjoy touching them, running your fingers through their hair, holding them, and following them with your eyes whilst they move around.

You must have the habit of holding your spouse not only in the privacy of your home but also in public. Especially, with women, they need emotional security. They want to feel loved. Hug your spouse a lot. Initiate to hold his or her hands, to kiss him or her, and to have the habit of tenderly squeezing his of her tokus or tooshie.

In Song of Solomon, the Shulamite speaks of her husband:

Let him kiss me with the kisses of his mouth…

Song of Solomon 1:2

Also in Song of Solomon 2:6, she goes further by saying, "his left hand is under my head, and his right hand embraces me…" This lady is indicating that she is enjoying the touch of her husband's hands.

If you are a woman who loves for romance to be expressed to you through touch, you must make sure your hot spots such as your posterior is well firmed and toned so he can enjoy it like a round ball in his palm when he feels it. Don't let yourself go that your backside is all fleshy and marshy.

Moreover, for the lady, if she yearns for romance through touch, depriving her of this will seriously and adversely affect how she functions at home, in the bedroom, and how she responds to you.

God has the following advise for every husband:

18 Let your fountain be blessed, and rejoice with the wife of your youth. 19 As a loving deer and   a graceful doe, <u>let her breasts satisfy you at all times</u>; And always be enraptured with her love

Proverbs 5:18-19

How To Identify Your Spouse's <u>Romance Language</u>

Remember, romance language is a type of verbal and non-verbal communication that easily titillates, stimulates and turns your spouse on. In this section, I want to show you ways to identifying your spouse's romance language. A husband and wife who make it a conscious effort to express all seven simultaneously will without fail have a wonderful, heavenly marriage.

(I) For the romance language of the tongue

Try affirming him or her by using kind words, and see how he or she responds. Always give her eye contact when she speaks or when you speak to her. For example: anytime your wife feeds you, look at her and thank her for the meal and let her know how you enjoyed it, and see how she responds. If it brightens her face and demeanor and it transcends to the bedroom: that could be her romance language, and if that is her romance language, you must use this often.

Compliment what she wears. Thank her when she takes care of your sexual and concupiscence needs. Tell her often that you love her and frequently tell her she is the best thing that happened to you. After all, when someone does you a favor or does what is required of them on the job for you, even if the person is your subordinate, don't you thank them? How much more your spouse? When your significant other does you a favor, and even does what is required of him or her, still express appreciation. It's not only a sign of civilization but also a sign of appreciation.

(II) For the romance language of time

If your spouse asks to go out, asks to be taken to the movies, an event, a restaurant, a party etc, and does this often, his or her love language might be a longing to always spend valuable, precious time with you. If he or she always wants to talk to you, to be by you, and so forth, that might be his or her love language. You will also know if your spouse's romance language is quality time if asking them out elates and excites them.

(III) For the romance language of treasures

If your spouse complains that you don't care, his or her love language might be a craving for you to show him or her that you care. If buying him or her gifts, sending text messages, love notes, flowers, and emails make his or her day, your spouse's romance language might be you showing that you care.

(IV) For the romance language of talents

Remember that if your spouse sees romance in terms of you maximizing your potential and rising to become all that you were born to be, and having the privilege of sharing in your success, finding out what your unique talents and gifts are will be the main difference maker in your marriage. The way to finding out what your unique gifts and talents are is by using principles such as the ones below:

(a) The principle of enquiry

Anyone who wants to find out what talents God has placed in them must apply the principle of enquiry. The principle of enquiry makes you conduct a systematic investigation and search. This systematic investigation and search for the knowledge of one's talents is done through prayer and asking God simple questions such as:

- What am I here for?

  _____

  _____

  _____

- Why was I created?

  _____

  _____

  _____

- What can I do productively?

  _____

  _____

  _____

(b) The principle of enthusiasm

Another principle to apply in your quest to finding out what talents God has placed in you is the principle of enthusiasm. Enthusiasm has to do with pursuing what gives you the highest level of excitement. It is asking yourself questions such as:

- What am I keenly interested in?

  _____

  _____

  _____

- What do I have the zeal for?

  _____

  _____

  _____

- What am I passionate about?

  _____

  _____

  _____

(c) The principle of enjoyment

Another principle you can apply in your pursuit of finding your unique talents is the principle of enjoyment. There is definitely some thing that come to you naturally, which you also enjoy doing. By enjoyment, you must ask yourself questions such as:

- What gives me the maximum gratification?

  _____

  _____

  _____

- What gives me the utmost pleasure?

  _____

  _____

  _____

- What gives me the greatest fulfillment?

_____

_____

_____

(d) The principle of effectiveness

The last principle you can use to find out what your unique talents are is the principle of effectiveness. God wants you to succeed and that is why He placed gifts, talents and strengths in you. You were not born to just get by, live an average or below average life. You were born to live an above average life and the key to living an above average life is by you locating and cultivating, discovering and developing, and finding and following your unique gifts and talents. By effectiveness, you must ask yourself questions such as:

- What do I find myself more useful doing?

_____

_____

_____

- What do I do best within the shortest possible time?

_____

_____

_____

- What do I do getting greater results with ease?

_____

_____

_____

Everyone has an innate, unique talent from God and it's your responsibility to find out what yours is, and then develop and maximize it to bless humanity. The person who without doubt will be the primary beneficiary is your spouse, and if this is the romance language your spouse understands, you will be doing your marriage a great service just by finding and following your talents.

(V) For the romance language of thinking

If your wife gives you the utmost attention when you speak and has his or her eyes fixed on you and she has the expression of being awed by what you say, using your thinking prowess might be his or her romance language. If your spouse encourages you through academics and other means to improve yourself knowledge-wise, it might be because he or she enjoys you and feels romance coming out of you when you speak.

(VI) For the romance language of teamwork

If your spouse feels disappointed and irate when you disregard him or her in decision-making, his or her romance language might by a craving of being treated as a partner and a coequal. Relating to your spouse as a teammate is necessary to the stability and steadiness of your marriage.

(VII) For the romance language of touch

You will know if your spouse's romance language is touch if he or she doesn't want to let go of you right away when you hug. If your spouse's language she responds to sexually is bodily touch, you will notice she enjoys foreplay more than intercourse because she gets to be touched, caressed, smooched and fondled and for her that is where love is expressed the most.

If your spouse also directs your hand as to where to stroke and touch during lovemaking, it might be (1) a hint of where her most sensitive and hot spot is, and (2) a hint that her romance language is bodily touch. Hence, she is directing your hand to do more touching and at the right spots.

I recommend for every husband and wife to commit to consciously and deliberately express romance in all the seven ways I have discussed: tongue, time, treasures, talents, thinking, teamwork and touch. This will provide you with a balanced and a healthy love life at home.

Marriage Matters

Chapter 8

The Power Of Sex

*T*hough the word sex is not found in the Bible, especially in the old and original translations, the Bible implicitly and candidly talks about it. A good example is Genesis 2:24, where it says, "a man shall leave his father and mother and shall cleave to his wife: and they shall become one flesh." Do you understand the term "one flesh?"

When a man and woman marry they do not become one flesh. *The only time oneness in flesh occurs is during sexual intercourse because at that time the man is in the woman and the two at that point become one flesh.* Hence, one flesh is synonymous to sexual intercourse.

God inspired the authors of the Bible to use metaphoric language to reference it. For instance, in Genesis 4:1, you read the words; "And Adam knew his wife and she conceived..."

Please take note of the phrase "Adam knew his wife." Does it mean that all this while Adam did not know his wife?" Secondly, how could knowing someone lead to conception? This is referring to sex.

Therefore, the Bible is not at all silent on the topic of sex and we don't have to be silent on it either. For us as believers, we can't afford to wallow in the pool of ignorance since it's our God who created this act and bond. If God created it and if the Bible freely discusses it, and as a representative of God on earth, I don't see why I should not freely share the information in this book to correct every wrong myth, and to uproot every deep rooted ignorance that is keeping people blind from freely expressing themselves in the bedroom.

Biblical Perspective of Sex

(1) Sex Is God-Ordained

Sex is God's idea and if it's God's idea, it means it's of a divine origin. Remember the one who said in Genesis 2:24 that "a man shall leave his father and mother and shall cleave to his wife: and they shall become one flesh," is God.

Since God is the one who instituted sexual union, it makes sex God-ordained and of a divine origin.

Since sex is God-ordained, it is a pure act. That is why in Hebrews 13:4, the Bible tells us "the marriage bed must be kept pure." If the act is a pure, holy act, you should be at liberty to invite the presence of God to saturate the atmosphere during the act, and even to ask Him in prayer to help you enjoy the act. Furthermore, as a purposeful God and creator, we know He created our sexual organs not for fun, but for a purpose, which is for sexual activity.

(2) Sex Is Permissible Only In Marriage

The next thing to know about sex is that it is permissible only in marriage. In Genesis 2:24, did you notice that God spoke of "one flesh" after He had said: "therefore shall a man leave his father and mother and cleave to his wife, then they shall become one flesh."

So "one flesh" which means sexual union only takes place in marriage. If you are not married and you engage in the act, you're violating biblical and spiritual order, and if you are married and you indulge in the act outside of marriage, you are again violating biblical and spiritual order. The former is a sin, which God calls fornication, and the latter is also a sin, He calls adultery. *In God's eyes, marriage is the only institution that makes sex acceptable and legal.*

(3) Sex Is Very Good

In Genesis 1:31, the Bible tells us that when God saw everything He had created (everything including the moon, stars, sun, animals, mankind, sex etc), He said it was "very good." He didn't just say it was good, but very good!

In the sight of God, sex is very good and it is for married people only. For those who are married, just think about some of the advantages of having sex: the psychological benefits such as it being a stress reliever; the health benefits such as increased heart rate, increased pulse rate and the physiology one goes through, and the fulfillment of scripture. *God doesn't create bad stuff and He sure was on spot when He created sex.*

(4) Sex Is To Be Enjoyed

The next thing to know about sex is that, it is to be enjoyed. For some married couples, their sex lives are boring. Some men in bed are like Onan. They only like to take care of themselves and do not look out for the interest of their wives, which is what Onan did to Tamar (Genesis 38:9). After they selfishly take care of themselves, they are not able to help the lady climb up because of the compulsory resolution stage they plateau into.

Sex in marriage can grow cold when you permit it. A lady must know what it means to seduce her man with scents, appearance and so forth. Ladies, make yourselves attractive at all times. Your lingerie, makeup and intimate apparel must be irresistible. *Make yourself in such a way that when your husband sees you, he can't help it but to want to come around you.* In Proverbs 5:18, we are admonished to "...rejoice with the wife of our youth." This scripture is encouraging every man to enjoy life, including sex with his wife.

(5) Sex Is For Procreation

Another biblical perspective of sex is that it is ordained by God as a means of procreation. After God created Adam and formed Eve, He gave them a mandate in Genesis 1:28 "…to be fruitful and multiply and fill the earth…" This shows that sex is the means through which children are made to fill the earth.

(6) Sex Is For A Man And A Woman

The next thing to know about sex is that God intended it to be between a man and a woman, and not between a man and a man or a woman and a woman or a human and an animal. Notice that in Genesis 2:24, God said, "therefore a man shall leave his father and mother and be joined to his wife…" Notice here that God intends for a man to join a wife (woman) in marriage.

God ordained and created sex and He intended for it to be between a man and a woman who are married. This is not my opinion but what the Word of God says. *According to God's Word, not my opinion, same sex marriage or sex between people of the same gender is unacceptable and a violation of biblical order.* This is not what I think; it's what God's Word says.

Paul has this to say of the subject:

> [26] *Because people did those things, God left them and let them do the shameful things they wanted to do.*

Women stopped having natural sex and started having sex with other women.

27 In the same way, men stopped having natural sex and began wanting each other. Men did shameful things with other men...

Romans 1:26-27 (NCV)

(7) Sex Is God's Gift To Man

A gift is something you did nothing to deserve yet it was given to you. A gift is something that is freely given for your exclusive pleasure. When God thought of marriage, He thought of giving married couples the pleasure of enjoying this great gift, and that is why no husband and wife should feel bound to fully express themselves sexually in the bedroom.

Keep this in mind: a gift is something you did not deserve yet it was given to you for you to freely enjoy. In subsequent chapters, I will delve into how you can enjoy this heavenly gift of sex.

Chapter 9

10 Things A Woman Wants In The Bedroom

In this chapter I want to show you ten basic things every wife wants in the bedroom. If you want your marriage to sizzle, if you want to keep love alive and if you want to maintain a continual happy mood at home, ensure you are well vested in these areas.

(1) A Romantic Man

Every woman wants a romantic man. Every wife wants her husband to be a man who is kind and affectionate. *Every wife appreciates a husband who takes the time to carefully identify what she sees as romantic and makes it a point to consciously communicate her romance language to her frequently.* Solomon identified what his wife considered

75

romantic, and he specifically communicated and expressed it over and over to her. To find out how to identify your spouse's romance language, refer to chapter 7.

(2) A Man With Staying Power

Every wife doesn't appreciate a husband who has a problem with premature ejaculation. When you have a problem with premature ejaculation, your lady will come to a point where she is afraid to freely let go of herself because she psychologically feels you will make her climb up and toward orgasm drop and disappoint her.

There are techniques to overcoming premature ejaculation and the workable ones if not medical are:

(a) Pull Out Push In Technique

The basic technique is the pull out and put back in technique. This is when the man toughens his mind to stop thrusting, pulls out to lose momentum and to delay orgasm and then reinserts to resume thrusting. This technique works for some men since they are able to delay orgasm and are able to remain firm for further stimulation of the clitoris whilst thrusting.

(b) Squeeze Technique

The squeeze technique requires that you work with your wife in the process. The whole idea is to delay orgasm and subsequently prolong the sexual experience. With this technique, what you do is to announce to your wife when you feel you're about to ejaculate, and when you pull out she will then hold the lower shaft of your penis and squeeze it gently for about five seconds.

She will do this by placing her thumb on the frenulum and her first and second fingers on the opposite side. This will effectively abort ejaculation. With this, you can resume thrusting till she is able to experience sexual climax ahead of you.

(c) Sensate Focus Technique

This is a technique in which the couple engages in non-genital caressing. With this you don't focus on your own pleasure but the focus is on the pleasure of your wife. Since women can easily experience sexual climax during foreplay or the excitement phase of the human sexual response cycle, the man is encouraged to give sexual pleasure to his wife without attempting intercourse. This is done to help the woman to have orgasm ahead of the man.

(d) Breathing Technique

Breathing right is not only good for sports and singing but very helpful for lovemaking. Every strength trainer will tell you that there is a direct correlation between how you breathe and the strength exuded to lift or push a weight. Every voice trainer will also tell you there is a direct connection between how you breathe and how you modulate and pitch musically. Similarly, a man who is able to coordinate and control his breathing will be able to stay longer in bed. In thrusting, the man must learn the method of breathing in when he pushes down and breathing out when he comes up. The ability to coordinate this movement with your inhalation and exhalation will assist the man in delaying sexual climax.

(3) A Selfless Man

Women don't like to feel used. They do not like a husband whom after he's experienced orgasm, turns around and seeks his pillow to sleep. *Every woman wants a man who continues to hold, touch and stroke her although he's moved to the resolution stage.*

(4) A Gentleman

Women don't like to be forced into sex. Yes, most of them want you to dominate and lead, but none of them want to give admission and the right of entry through compulsion and duress. Although they don't report it to the authorities, forcing your lady is seen as rape. Generally, they like to be allured and gently attracted and ushered into the mood. A man must learn how to set the right mood and gently allure his wife into the mood.

(5) A Man Who Seek Her Interest

Women are interested in men who seek their sexual fulfillment. They want you to bring them to orgasm, and they also want you to take pride and pleasure cleaning all the fluid and juices that are secreted during sex.

(6) A Man With A Well-Trained Tongue

Okay, I know what you're thinking now. That she wants you to get down on her. Maybe! But more than that, there's something else she wants. Every woman wants a man who uses his tongue to give her compliments. She wants to be told: "You are beautiful," "You are so sexy," "I love your cheek dimples," "Your eyes are beautiful," "You are the best thing that happened to me."

(7) A Full-Body Lovemaking

If you're a man who wants to be perceived as a great lover, you must do more than get your pleasure and move on. For women, sex starts in their mind. So take the extra time to romance your woman with soft music, sweet scents and stroke her all over the body.

Once you touch her, caress her entire body before even touching her hot spots like her nipples and inner thighs. Take your time to fondle her in less obvious places like her neck, palm and behind the ears.

(8) A Leader Without Inhibitions

She wants you to take the lead and maintain the space for her to surrender to you enjoying her. Nothing is more masculine than taking the lead and showing that you have direction, and you know what you want and you're going for it.

For example, the most common sexual fantasy for women is to be dominated in bed. Take her hands and place them over her head while you kiss her neck and whisper and talk to her. Avoid asking questions. Not in bed. Ever. In bed, nothing turns off a woman more than being asked, do you want me to kiss you on the neck? Should I take off your blouse? Would you like me to go slow? Dude, just take charge and take the lead!

(9) A Good Sexual Performance

Unless mean, most women will never say anything to indicate that you are small. Why? Because they don't want to hurt you by making you feel inadequate. In most cases, size is more of an issue in the mind of men, who fret over the size of their organ.

However, you should know that women don't care nearly as much about penile size as they do about performance. *By performance, I mean stiffness, thrusting and lasting power.* When it comes to men's sexual performance, what women want in bed is to avoid going through the embarrassment of a weak erection or of a premature ejaculation.

(10) A Safe Haven

Every woman wants a man with whom she feels safe. She wants to be in bed with a man whom she knows wont hurt her but respects and loves her. Not a man who puts her down and abuses her verbally and/or physically.

Marriage Matters

Chapter 10

10 Things A Man Wants In The Bedroom

In this chapter I want to show you ten basic wants of husbands in the bedroom. If you're a wife, wanting your marriage to sizzle and desiring a constant, ceaseless happy mood at home, read this section attentively.

(1) An Exciting Woman

In general, men want their wives to be excited about sex. No husband likes to beg or force his wife to have sex. Also men want wives who show enthusiasm about sex, wives who look forward to the act, and subsequently make it a thrilling experience for herself and her husband. A woman who fails to express positive emotions or maintain eye contact after penetration is a source of displeasure for her husband.

(2) An Involving Woman

Men also want women who are involved in the sexual activities of foreplay and intercourse. Not the kind of woman who lies down as though she were a piece of wood as her husband touches and thrusts her. Even when you are mad at him, the act is sacred and pure, so have the fear of God's presence on your marriage bed, and approach it with awe and reverence.

In Song of Solomon 7:10, the Shulamite says, "I am my beloved's, and his desire is toward me." Over here, she implies that, because I always involve myself with my husband, his desire is always toward me.

(3) An Adventurous Woman

Men want wives who give them variety and a range of positions in the bedroom. By variety, I mean a woman who is open and suggestive of different lovemaking techniques and positions other than the usual man-on-top style of lovemaking. Every husband appreciates exploration and adventurous sex.

(4) A Humble Woman

Men also prefer women who are full of humility – wives who willingly surrender themselves to them without resistance and struggle. Being modest and looking out for your spouse's happiness is key to marital success.

As a wife, you must know what it means to willingly surrender yourself to your husband, doing whatever he says, rolling willingly, spreading your legs open freely and readily hold him tightly without being told. He craves for you so always give him the best lovemaking experience. Give him a good kiss and startle him with your humility.

Solomon says of his wife that, "your lips, O my spouse drip like honeycomb; honey and milk are under your tongue..." (Song of Solomon 4:11). Solomon is talking about his wife freely kissing him back because she's aware her tongue is as sweet as honey. Married woman, don't let tradition and any form of unfounded taboo on sex education stop you from having fun sticking your tongue into your husband's mouth and sucking his tongue like it's a lollipop. Your man will love that and you will be doing your marriage lots of favor as you make your husband happy in the bedroom.

(5) A Cooperative Woman

Every wife must have the habit of willingly stripping herself naked without being told. Without feeling subjugated and enslaved, she must take pleasure fulfilling her husband's sexual fantasies so the enemy doesn't set him up for another woman to meet those needs. Don't be a woman who refuses to strip. Sex is part of the package of marriage and when it's boring, the marriage potentially could fail.

(6) A Full of Surprise Woman

Men like to be surprised especially in the bedroom. If you want to touch your husband's heart and want him to say yes to a request of yours that probably involves a huge expense, surprise him! Surprise him and turn him on especially with scents and perfumes. The Shulamite was good at that in her marriage to Solomon. Solomon talked of her ability to surprise her in the following verse:

> *How fair is your love,*
> *My sister, my spouse!*
> *How much better than wine is your love,*
> *And the scent of your perfumes than all spices!*

> *Song of Solomon 4:10*

Can you imagine your husband coming home from work and by the time he enters the bedroom, you are wearing an alluring intimate apparel, soft music is playing in the background, an erotic candle is lit, your body is soaked with the enchanting aroma of your perfumes, the bed is well dressed with four scarves, each positioned at the corner of the bed.

Before he says anything, you tell him, "honey, go have a shower, your juicy juice is waiting for you." Do you know what will be happening inside him? His hypothalamus will be unleashed. His libido will be charged, and he will run to the shower like he is being chased by a mad dog, and when he returns, he finds you naked on the bed with your hands and leg stretched open, then you whisper "tie my hands and legs with each scarf. I am all yours tonight."

Can you imagine what will happen? Men love surprises. He will feel charged, provoked and empowered for action. May God help you to get creative in the bedroom! No need to let the devil make you feel uneasy and uncomfortable over the distilled truths in this book. It is biblically based. More so, I want to help you succeed in marriage and if I can help you to get creative to enjoy the union, I believe God would be thrilled you did not take His creation for granted because you were wise enough to be fruitful in this regard.

(7) A Playful Woman

By nature, men function on their ego. Because of that, they tend to want their wives to boost their ego. Every wife who celebrates her man's manhood and masculinity will always boost his ego. As a wife you must have the habit of being playful with him, including playing with his genitals.

You should be able to hold his phallus with your hands wrapped around it, whilst you strip him nude on the bed, and as you stir at his pileus, you tell him: you are a strong man. You are the best thing that ever happened to me. I won't trade this for nothing. Do you know what you would be doing to him? You would be sending his ego, self-image, self-worth and opinion of himself skyrocketing through the roof, and guess what? It will make your marriage sizzle.

(8) An Inviting Woman

Men want wives who willingly invite them for lovemaking. You can do this by what you say, how you walk in front of him and so forth. You can also stroke him on his buttocks whilst he walks by or send him an email or a text message whilst he is at work to indicate to him that you crave his body and that his fresh and hot lover girl desires for him. Learn to invite your man for bedroom works.

In Song of Solomon 4:16, you read the following words from the Shulamite: "let my beloved come to his garden and eat its pleasant fruits." This is a clear invitation to her husband to come make love with her. Do you know what garden represents here? Do you know what eating it's pleasant fruits represent? Figure it out!

(9) A Frequent Sex-Giving Woman

One of the things men want more of, is sex. This is because no normal man can do without it. Sex is a primary need of a man, and a need is reminiscent of a necessity. A necessity is something you can't do without. No real, healthy man can do without sex. Your husband will be very glad if you cultivate the habit of being ready for more frequent sex. An average man wants sex at least on two separate nights. A wife should never use sex as a weapon to punish her man. Even if he has angered you: seek a resolution right away and get together again.

There are women who use sex as a weapon to punish or get back at their husbands, and the excuses men complain they use are: I am tired, I am not in the mood, and I don't feel like it. When you withhold sex from your spouse, someone else outside your marriage will be willing to give to your husband that which you're withholding from him, and that is when an affair starts. So keep this in mind: when you withhold sex from your spouse, you are in effect encouraging your spouse to go look for it outside the marriage.

In First Corinthians 7: 5, the Bible says "don't deprive yourselves of sex except it be with consent so that Satan does not tempt you for your inconsistency." Prior to this, the Bible says in the verse 4 that "the wife does not have power over her own body, but the husband: and likewise the husband does not have power over his own body but the wife." This means that when your spouse feels for you, even when you're tired, you must exit the realm of tiredness and enter into the corridor of romance to meet his sexual needs.

Although he is to understand when you say you are tired, if he is still craving for your body, the above Scripture instructs the wife to cooperate. By this, you will be helping your spouse not to look for sex outside the matrimonial home. If you are wise enough to not want to drive your spouse to another woman, don't withhold sex from him.

(10) A Feedback Woman

Remember, this section is only focusing on what men want in the bedroom, and not what they want in a marriage.

As I mentioned earlier, one of the primary needs of a man in the bedroom is sex and when it's given to him, he yearns for his wife to also verbally give him feedback of what he is doing.

Men expect their wives to talk, make sounds, touch them back and appreciate them as they thrust and make love. God gave you the ability be free on your marriage bed. Therefore, let go of yourself and make all the unintelligible sounds you can think of. There's nothing wrong with that!

From the poetic dialogue between Solomon and the Shalamite, we see lots of feedback in their marriage and bedroom affairs. For instance, in Song of Solomon 2:2-3, Solomon tells his wife, she is "like a lily among thorns, so is my love among the daughters." Then she gives her feedback and says, "like an apple tree among the trees of the woods, so is my beloved among the sons...and his fruit was sweet to my taste."

The Shulamite clearly was giving her feedback to Solomon that his fruit was sweet to her taste. This cannot be overemphasized. Men want signals that point to the fact that they are doing the right thing. Thus, get into the mood and freely let yourself go. It's beneficial not just to him but also to you.

<u>Results Of Sex Deprivation</u>

The risks of sex deprivation in marriage includes:

(1) Adulterous Acts

The greatest risk of marital sex deprivation is adultery. Although the parties involved have no excuse to be unfaithful, couples need to be made aware that the best way to avoid infidelity in their marriage is to satisfy each other sexually. Every couple should build a good, deep sexual life so as to avoid infidelity.

(2) Lascivious Acts

Apart from adultery, marital sex deprivation promotes other sexual immoralities such as masturbation, incest and rape. Though sexual denial should not be a basis for these kinds of sexual perversion, good and exciting sex in a marriage may help to avoid these sins.

(3) Temperamental Acts

Emotional outbursts are common in a marriage where sex is deprived and withheld from a spouse. Men are known to take it angrily when their wives deny them sex. They see it as a rejection of their manhood so they do not take it lightly. Denial of sex does lead to anger and strife. To avoid these aggravated feelings, women should learn to satisfy their men. Husbands also should learn to be civil and considerate when their wives cannot meet their sexual needs.

(4) Frustrating Acts

Sex deprivation leads to frustration. This can lead to crisis at home. It can also lead to bitterness, malice and resentment. This should be prevented as much as possible. Sex deprivation more often leads to bad marriages because it is a common cause of marital tension, that also leads to breakdown of communication, and the eventual decline of love, passion and romance in the marriage.

Chapter 11

33 Secrets Of An Irresistible Wife

*A*n irresistible wife is the kind of woman who is complete in herself. She is the type of woman every man dreams of having as a wife. She is the woman the Bible describes in Proverbs 31. To be a sassy, attractive, appealing wife: a lady whose husband can't help but to want to come around her all the time, you must desire to be like the woman described in the following:

10   *A wife of noble character who can find? She is worth far more than rubies.*
11   *Her husband has full confidence in her and lacks nothing of value.*
12   *She brings him good, not harm, all the days of her life.*
13   *She selects wool and flax and works with eager hands.*

93

14   *She is like the merchant ships, bringing her food from afar.*

15   *She gets up while it is still dark; she provides food for her family*

and portions for her servant girls.

16   *She considers a field and buys it; out of her earnings she plants a vineyard.*

17   *She sets about her work vigorously; her arms are strong for her tasks.*

18   *She sees that her trading is profitable, and her lamp does not go out at night.*

19   *In her hand she holds the distaff and grasps the spindle with her fingers.*

20   *She opens her arms to the poor and extends her hands to the needy.*

21   *When it snows, she has no fear for her household; for all of them are clothed in scarlet.*

22   *She makes coverings for her bed; she is clothed in fine linen and purple.*

23   *Her husband is respected at the city gate,*

where he takes his seat among the elders of the land.

24   *She makes linen garments and sells them, and supplies the merchants with sashes.*

25   *She is clothed with strength and dignity; she can laugh at the days to come.*

26   *She speaks with wisdom, and faithful instruction is on her tongue.*

27   *She watches over the affairs of her household and does not eat the bread of idleness.*

28   *Her children arise and call her blessed; her husband also, and he praises her:*

29   *"Many women do noble things, but you surpass them all."*

30   *Charm is deceptive, and beauty is fleeting;*

but a woman who fears the LORD is to be praised.

³¹   *Give her the reward she has earned, and let her works bring her praise at the city gate.*

Proverbs 31:10-31

An irresistible woman is the lady who…

Spiritual Level

(1) Knows How To Be Noble

An irresistible woman has a noble character. She has high moral qualities and approves of only things that are excellent. In other words, she looks at the difference between good and bad and chooses the good over the bad. So the question in Proverbs 31:10 is, *"A wife of noble character who can find?"* An irresistible wife possesses a noble character.

(2) Knows How To Worship And Praise God

She has passion and love in her heart for God. This makes her enjoy expressing who God is and what God has done for her. She is aware that life without God is empty and a marriage without God is frustrating.

(3) Knows How To Reverence God

She lives to please God. Therefore, she has the fear of God in her and would not do that which renders her as not reverencing God. She is aware of Proverbs 1:7 that the fear of the Lord leads to wisdom, but despising the Lord is an act of foolishness. So she keeps God in her marriage and introduces His precepts and principles to her children.

(4) Knows How To Be Christ-Like

She strives to want to be like Jesus. She prays for her husband and children and she prays aloud so her husband knows he is being prayed for. Her prayer entreats the Lord to protect, provide and prosper her family, thus assuring her husband that he has complete spiritual support.

(5) Knows How To Be Sincere

An irresistible wife is a sincere lady. She is transparent, honest, truthful and blameless. She plays no secretive games with her man because sincerity is her way of life.

She has reverence for God and deliberately chooses right over wrong when presented with the alternative. In Proverbs 31:11, the Bible describes her as a wife whose "husband safely trusts her."

(6) Knows How To Be Chaste

That is, she keeps herself pure. She is not only a woman of high moral standards, but also a true virtuous woman. Issues of unfaithfulness do not run through her mind.

She is simply pure and chaste, doing her man no evil. Proverbs 31:12 affirm this virtue by saying, "she does him good and not evil all the days of her life."

Emotional Level

(7) Knows How To Seduce And Entice Her Man

Even when her husband is tired, an irresistible woman knows how to lure her man to even forget about his tired body and get to work. An irresistible woman seduces her husband. As a result her man is consumed with her all the time. She just knows how to turn him on.

(8) Knows How To Make Love To Her Husband

Because of her, sex is never boring on her marital and matrimonial bed. She is adventurous; she moves; she touches; she holds; she just makes lovemaking the best activity next to worshipping God. She is involving and exciting in bed. She is not shy to make the first move in bed. She sets the mood, which allows things to happen.

(9) Knows How To Care For Her Man

She cares for her man and is concerned for him. She knows how to love her children and she is like a hen to her children - a hen who fights for her chicks, protecting, providing and caring for them. Proverbs 31:15 describe an irresistible wife as a woman who "provides food for her household." By providing food for her household, she is being portrayed as a man who cares for her husband and children.

(10) Knows How To Satisfy Her Husband's Emotional And Sexual Needs

An irresistible woman knows that her body belongs to her husband. She never views withholding sex as a tool for getting back at or punishing her husband. She is willing to make love to her husband to meet his sexual needs and have him meet her sexual needs as well.

Personal Level

(11) Knows How To Dress

An irresistible woman is excellent at coordinating her colors and outfits. She is good at wearing what allures her husband because she is a sharp dresser. She knows what to wear to turn her husband on and make him proud of her. Even if she wears rugs, she still looks good in it. She does not see beauty as an external expression only but as an internal feeling that is expressed outwardly.

(12) Knows How To Cook

This is the woman who finds out what her man likes to eat and prepares that for him often. She is aware that the way to a man's heart is sometimes through his stomach so she concerns herself with what her man eats. This is the woman who doesn't wait to be told to prepare food. She offers it without being asked.

(13) Knows How To Talk

Speaks to her man gently and she never raises her voice at him. She is a lady and talks like a lady. No foul language proceeds from her mouth. She sees it as a sin to argue with or raise her voice at her husband, the priest and head of the house. She is aware of the spiritual authority God has placed on the man and as such submits to her man's spiritual authority.

(14) Knows How To Walk

She walks like a lady and not like a man or a villager. She walks with her chest out and never with her head bowed. She is a woman you could take anywhere, knowing you would not be embarrassed. She will enthrall, captivate and wow her onlookers.

(15) Knows How To Take Advise

Whether constructive or not she takes every advise in good faith. She is aware that in the multitude of advice there is safety. She also is cognizant that all she knows is all she has learnt, and all she has learnt is all she knows, and that there is a lot more she doesn't know yet.

(16) Knows How To Be Hygienic

She is a clean person both outwardly and inwardly. Her hair is always clean, and her nails and toes have excellent manicure and pedicure respectively. She's always clean and ready for her man.

(17) Knows How To Be Charming

This woman has an attractiveness that interests, pleases and stimulates her man. She is referred to as sassy or what the world calls sexy. She is just hot and fresh. Her very presence alone makes her man to want to be all over her and even crawl into her if possible.

(18) Knows How To Be Excellent

Excellence is her way of life. She does things to the best of her ability. She gives out her best in everything she does. Proverbs 31:29 describes her in these words: "Many daughters have done well, but you excel them all."

Sacrificial Level

(19) Knows How To Sow

She is a generous giver and supporter of God's work. She believes in sowing and reaping. She knows that where your heart is there your treasure will be (Matthew 6:21). Therefore, because her heart is for God she makes her treasure go to God. As she does this, she knows she is applying a principle that will also make her man's heart and treasure always be with her.

(20) Knows How To Be Benevolent

She supports the poor, needy and disadvantaged. She is benevolent and not at all stingy. According to Proverbs 31:20, an irresistible wife is the kind who "extends her hand to the poor, yes, she reaches out her hands to the needy." This is referring to her being benevolent.

(21) Knows How To Be Kindhearted

She is like Ruth who is willing to fetch water for Boaz when Boaz has not asked for water. She feels the needs of her lover and meets those needs accordingly. In Proverbs 31:20, we learn that she is not only benevolent but she stretches her hand to the needy to indicate she is kindhearted. Proverbs 31:26 also affirm, "on her tongue is the law of kindness."

(22) Knows How To Serve

She is humble enough to be a servant and at the same time a lady, a lover, a wife and a mother. She serves well at home and finds every opportunity to make a difference in the lives of her husband and children. Since an irresistible wife has the heart of a servant, Proverbs 31:17 says, "she girds herself with strength, and strengthens her arms." She does this due to her readiness to serve.

(23) Knows How To Be A Lady Of Integrity

Character matters to her more than reputation. She is aware that reputation is what people think you are whereas character is who you really are. Proverbs 31:10 show that because she is a woman of integrity, "her worth is above rubies."

Household Level

(24) Knows How To Keep A House

An irresistible wife is good at housekeeping. She cleans and tidies the house and constantly ensures her home is tidy. Proverbs 31:27 describe her as a woman who "watches over the ways of her household."

(25) Knows How To Make A Home

An irresistible wife turns a house to a home. She maintains a peaceful, calm, loving, playful and romantic atmosphere at home at all times. She is not hostile to her man and children. She is reminded of Proverbs 21:19 that it is "better to dwell in the wilderness, than with a contentious and angry woman."

(26) Knows How To Be Mindful Of Her Own Business

She stays away from other people's business. She does not poke her nose into other people's matters. She is not a gossip or a talebearer. She does not involve herself with other people's matters. She also does not talk about others and does not allow people to talk to her about others. She is aware that he who talks to you about others, talks to others about you, and as such gives no room for gossip.

Economic/Commercial Level

(27) Knows How To Be Industrious

She is business minded. She does not want her home to lack financially so she thinks in terms of profit, investment, increase, fruitfulness and productivity. Proverbs 31:13 describe her as a woman who "willingly works with her hands."

(28) Knows How To Be Financially Supportive Of Her Household

She is supportive and helpful. She knows how to bring extra income if the need be to support the home. She is described in Proverbs 31:24 as someone who "makes linen garments and sells them" to support her home. In other words, she brings in an additional stream of income to support her husband.

Miscellaneous Level

(29) Knows How To Be Loyal

She is like an eagle who mates with the same partner for life. She does not give room to anyone to interfere with her marriage. Divorce and adultery are not in her vocabulary. She is faithful to her man and to her children. Simply, she is a woman who protects her turf.

(30) Knows How To Earn Her Man's Trust

She is trustworthy and worthy of her man's trust. According to Proverbs 31:11, her husband has full confidence in her.

(31) Knows How To Be Diligent

She is hardworking and detail oriented. She is not at all lazy or shoddy. She understands that laziness is not part of her DNA, and as such is industrious and productive.

(32) Knows How To Be Bold

She is courageous. She is not a coward but bold. She is strong and outgoing. She knows how to encourage and strengthen her man in his weakest moments.

(33) Knows How To Be Wise

She is intelligent, smart, well informed, brilliant, clever, and level headed. She thinks things through before she makes a decision. She doesn't act before she thinks but thinks before she acts.

Chapter 12

The Power Of Money

*A*part from love and sex, the next thing that can affect your marriage is money. Let's examine the following passage before we proceed:

> ^{23} *Then Jesus said to His disciples, "Assuredly, I say to you that it is hard for a rich man to enter the kingdom of heaven.* ^{24} *And again I say to you, it is easier for a camel to go through the eye of a needle than for a rich man to enter the kingdom of God."*
>
> *Matthew 19:23-24*

This passage has to do with a rich young ruler who asked Jesus what he must do to inherit eternal life. Jesus asked him to obey the commandments such as not committing murder, not committing adultery and not coveting a neighbor's wife.

The rich man responded that he has kept all the commandments and there is not a single one he has violated. Jesus then looked at him and said to him, if he truly wants eternal life, he should go and sell all that he possessed and give it to the poor. The man was disappointed when Jesus said that and he left His presence sorrowful because he had a great many possessions.

After the man's departure, Jesus turned to His disciples and said, "it is easier for a camel to go through the eye of a needle than for a rich man to enter the kingdom of God." Over here, it looks like Jesus was condemning rich people and those who have abundance of money. Because of this, many people have built negative and limiting beliefs about money. Though it may seem odd that anyone would have a negative disposition toward money, often we hold these limiting beliefs in our subconscious even from childhood.

Perhaps when you were young, you heard statements such as:

- Money is the root of all evil

- People with money are bad

- People with money are selfish and self-centered

- People with lots of money can't be spiritual

- People with lots of money can't be trusted

These messages from early childhood can actually sabotage and dilute your later financial success, because they subconsciously emit a vibration that's contrary to your conscious intentions.

Jesus' View On Money

In the above passage, Jesus was not condemning rich people or money. Neither was He commending poverty. This rich man whose actions precipitated this shocking statement thought he was a good and righteous observer of the law and therefore did not need salvation to enter God's kingdom. *Jesus' statement implied that, as long as the rich think they have everything and do not need to be saved, it would be hard for them to enter heaven's kingdom.* This wasn't an attack on money or wealth. Rather, it was an attack on the rich man's attitude toward salvation, the door to the kingdom of heaven.

Jesus would have been a hypocrite if His statement were an attack on money and rich people. It took a rich man to give Him a befitting burial. Also 2 Corinthians 8:9 describe Jesus as a rich man. Poverty is not good but money is good. Proverbs 14:22 tells us, "a poor man is despised by his own friends." Lack of money is one of the main factors for the high rate of divorce, robbery, murder and other crimes in our society.

So money is good. It is even better when it's a husband and a wife who posses it in abundance. It gets better when they have all the proper foundation for a successful marriage in place, and they have abundant money to acquire the things they want, take frequent vacations to disassociate from the stressors of life to bond and allow their hearts to be knitted together.

The Love For Money

For the love of money is a root of all kinds of evil, for which some have strayed from the faith in their greediness, and pierced themselves through with many sorrows.

1 Timothy 6:10

Paul writes to Timothy that the love of money is the root of all kinds of evil. It did not say money is the root of all kinds of evil. It said, "the love of money" or having a wrong relationship with money – that's evil! Love has a deep and tender feeling for a person, thing or cause. You don't need to develop a deep tender feeling for money. Only desire for it!

In Ecclesiastes 10:19, we again learn that, "…money answers everything." Apart from money being good, God in the above verse shows that it answers everything. The answer to good education for your children, the answer to paying off your debt, the answer to buying and paying off your house, and the answer to every material lack in your life is money. Do you know that a simple vacation can help avoid some of the fights between couples and subsequently change the mood at home for better? Taking time off to get away is a great stress reliever, but it takes money to answer this anomaly.

The Role Money Plays In A Marriage

As I have been stating throughout this book, there are three factors that impact marriages more than any other: love, sex and money. How we handle money often leads to happiness or conflict in a marriage. Money definitely matters for the success of every marriage and it can make or break a marriage. Below are the biblical perspectives of money in a marriage.

(1) Money Must Be Transparently Managed

Marriages succeed when there is financial transparency between husband and wife. One of the healthy reasons why two people in love should marry is the desire to share things in common, and one of the things you share in common is your money and resources. *Irrespective of whether or not one person makes more money than the other, finances have to be brought to the table and managed together.*

(2) Money Must Be Managed Wisely

Many people know how to make money but very few know how to manage their money wisely. If you want to have a happy marriage, make sure you manage your income, inflow and intake wisely. That requires setting a budget on how you spend. *The basics of family finance are budgeting, saving, investing and spending wisely.* Every couple must know and abide by these principles!

(a) Budget

Manage your home with a budget. Know how much comes in and how much goes out. Know how much is your tithe, how much goes to housing, utilities, groceries etc, and by all means live within your means. Figure out which expenses are not necessary and eliminate them.

Sample Family Budget

A good family budget should include the following prioritized order:

Total Monthly Income _____

Monthly Expenditure:

    Tithe (Put God First) _____

    Housing (Mortgage/Rent) _____

    Grocery (Food) _____

    Transport (Car note/Insurance/Gas) _____

    Utilities (Electricity, Gas, Water) _____

    Telephone (Cell or Landline) _____

    Miscellaneous _____

Total Monthly Expenditure _____

    Surplus/Deficit _____

These are the necessities that must appear on your family budget. Others such as cable television, high speed internet, and buying new clothes can be avoided. I have suggested to numerous couples to try going a whole year without buying new clothes nor changing their wardrobe if they are serious minded about increasing their reserve. It works out just fine for those willing to be frugal and to make the sacrifice.

Some of the advantages of a budget are that it enables you to live within your means, to eliminate unnecessary spending, to increase your reserve, and to keep you from coming up short at the end of the month.

(b) <u>Savings</u>

Ensure that a portion of every money you receive is set aside for unforeseen contingency. It is unacceptable to not have a family savings account. You must by all means have a savings account and no matter the pressure and temptation to tap into that money, refuse to touch what is tucked away.

(C) <u>Investment</u>

Good parents invest in the future of their children. Investing in the future of your children provides a leverage of financial security for them. No matter how much or how little you make, ensure each of your children from birth at least have a college fund.

Good parents leave an inheritance not just for their children but also for their children's children.

*A good **man** leaves an inheritance to his children's children, but the wealth of the sinner is stored up for the righteous.*

Proverbs 13:22

Over here, the Bible tells us that a good man leaves an inheritance not just for his children, but also for his children's children. In other words, a good man does not only think of himself, but thinks of his children and even grandchildren. The Bible is indicating to us that a good man thinks of posterity, and the word posterity means "future generations."

God Almighty wants us to live our lives not for us and not for our children alone but for posterity. Until you become the kind of person who thinks of posterity, God does not classify you as a good man.

Who Is A Good "Man?"

Let me make this correction before we proceed. The word *"man"* as used in Proverbs 13:22 does not necessarily refer to the male gender for three main reasons:

- Firstly, the word *"man"* is in italics. If you're a good student of the Bible you know that italics in the scriptures simply mean the italicized word is the translators own insertion to make the sentence sensible, and that the word was not originally in the sentence.

- Secondly, the word *"man"* may mean "mankind." Man does not necessarily refer to the male gender because the word 'man' is the Hebrew word 'adam," which means mankind. As you are aware mankind refers to persons or human beings, which can be either male or female.

- Thirdly, the word *"man"* may mean parents or grandparents. This is because children and grandchildren are mentioned in the verse, and it does not only take a man to produce children, but a man and woman – parents. Also it takes grandparents to have grandchildren.

So Proverbs 13:22 is not limited to men but to persons, human beings, parents and grandparents. So in place of a "good man," I can comfortably say a good person, or a good parent to include men and women.

The Mindset of A Good "Man"

(A) A Good Man Thinks God

A good man is called good because he has earned the title of being good, and that is why He is called good. According to Jesus there is no one to be called good but God.

So He said to him, "Why do you call Me good? No one is good but One, that is, God...

Matthew 19:17

If God is the only One to be called good, He will subsequently call you good when your focus and mind is on Him. In other words, when you live to please Him, and your children see the attributes of the Father God in you their earthly parents, you will be called good.

A child should be able to look at how his or her father and mother carries themselves and be able to see God in them. A parent who does not model God before his or her children is disqualified in attempting to teach his or her children the ways of a God they have not modeled and mimicked before their children. This is what I mean by "a good man thinks God." God preoccupies his or her thinking.

(B) A Good Man Thinks Family

Notice that children are mentioned in Proverbs 13:22 to imply that a good man thinks of his family. A good man cares about His family. In Job chapter 1, the unknown author of the book describes Job as a perfect, upright, God-fearing, good man. Do you know why Job was described as a good man? Because Job loved his family! Job's piety is made so evident that the author tells us that because of the wealth and inheritance he had amassed for himself and for his children, his children threw lots of parties. After every party Job sanctified his children and offered sacrifices to God to ask for forgiveness for his children just in case they've sinned against Him. Because of his love for family, the author describes him as a good man and the greatest of all the men of the East.

The principle is that a good man thinks family: loves his family; cares for his family; provides for his family; prays for his family.

(C) A God Man Thinks Inheritance

According to Proverbs 13:22, a good man leaves an inheritance for his children and grandchildren. A good man doesn't think short-term but long-term. A good man doesn't think of himself but beyond himself. He is not shortsighted but long-sighted. Doesn't just have sight but foresight.

To Leave an Inheritance Means…

- To leave a legacy
- To leave a memorial
- To leave a possession
- To leave a succession (a title, an estate or prosperity his children can benefit)
- To make a difference in the lives of others
- To make an indelible mark

The righteous man walks in his integrity;
His children are blessed after him.

Proverbs 20:7

Will whatever you are doing now allow you to leave a legacy? Do you have the mindset and the attitude of your children growing to be better off than you? *Your children must not grow to face the same struggles you're facing, and fight the same battles you're fighting.* They must be better off. Why? Because a good man leaves an inheritance: a legacy; a memorial; a possession, a succession for his children and children's children.

(D) A Good Man Thinks Posterity

In Proverbs 13:22, the Bible tells us that; "a good man leaves an inheritance to his children's children." The revelation is that a good man does not only think of himself and even his children only, but he thinks across generations. That is, a good man thinks trans-generational. He doesn't think of himself but thinks beyond his generation to the next generation (which is his children), and even to the next generation after his children (which is his grandchildren; the third generation). Hence, a good man thinks future generations, trans-generation, and posterity.

Children's children are the crown of old men,
And the glory of children is their father.

Proverbs 17:6

(3) Money Must Take Care of Your Family

Never allow your family to suffer: take good care of them, provide for them and make them comfortable. You should legitimately find other streams of income to sustain your family. You are not good parents, especially the father until you give your family real comfort. Make your family priority.

(4) Money Must Train Your Children

Your children's wellbeing particularly their schooling must be very important to you. Give your children sound education. Equip them with every tool they need to face the future and succeed. Give them what you didn't have and give them more than what you were given by your own parents.

Be personally involved in your children's education. Help them every night with their homework, be present at every school event of theirs, and send them a message that you love and care about them, and would do everything in your power to help them succeed. Get them the books they need and help them succeed academically. Always remember that education is the best gift and the lasting legacy you can give your children. Plan your children's academic future whilst they are young.

In a nutshell, team up as husband and wife, share ideas and plan your finances together so you can avoid financial pressure and meltdown, which has the potential to wreck your marriage.

Chapter 13

Common Causes Of Marital Tension

*W*hen finances are not managed well, and a spouse's romance language is not identified, and sex is withheld, the marriage will experience lots of problems. In this chapter, I want to show you some of the common causes of marital problems and how to avoid these common problems. Every problem in a marriage has its roots stemming from either one or a combination of the following:

When God is Ignored in the Marriage

If you take God out of the marriage, the union will struggle and eventually fail. You cannot keep the manufacturer of a product out of his creation and hope to have it to work efficiently and give you maximum satisfaction. The only legitimate person with the authority to fix or provide you with technical support regarding a product is the manufacturer of the product.

Similarly, as the institutor of marriage, you can't keep God out of His institution and hope to experience success. *God cannot be kept from the institution of marriage if you hope for marital success.* Let's examine this:

> [9] *Two are better than one, because they have a good reward for their labor...* [10] *But woe to him who is alone* ...[12] *A threefold cord is not quickly broken.*

> *Ecclesiastes 4:9-10,12*

I like how this Scripture ends. It says a threefold cord is not quickly broken. In a marriage, the husband represents the first cord. The wife represents the second cord, and God is the third cord that Ecclesiastes refers to. When you decide to tie a rope with two strands, the knot will easily be untied. However, when you decide to tie with three strands, it will be difficult for the knot to be untied. This is because with three strands, the first weaves around the second, the third and itself, and the second weaves around the first and itself and likewise the third.

God is that third cord in the marriage and when you allow Him to weave around the husband and the wife, the knot that will be tied around the marriage will be so strong; it will never be untied by any marital pressure or force. If you want your marriage to succeed, you must keep God in your marriage. You keep Him in the marriage by praying together, studying His Word together, and getting fed with His Word together so you both can grow together spiritually.

When There Are Intrusive Forces

Another common cause of marital tension is intrusive forces and that is when you allow external influences into your marriage. Intrusive forces can mean interference by in-laws, parents, and friends offering you advice concerning your marriage. If you want your marriage to succeed, you must consciously refrain from discussing your spouse with your friends, family, and especially your parents because they could offer you counsel that in the long run could be detrimental to your marriage. The reason is: they would particularly look out for your interest, not the interest of your marriage as a whole. After all, you're their child, and your spouse is technically not theirs. So they innately would look out for you first.

No matter what happens in your marriage, trust God to endow you with common sense to resolve it. Never discuss the problems at home with an outsider. By all means, keep your friends, siblings and parents out of your marriage. If the conflict is not being resolved, look for a trusted Christian professional or a pastor to seek counsel from them. No one likes for his or her dirty linen to be washed outside. So to avoid making your spouse feel you've been washing his or her dirty linen outside, keep whatever happens at home in the confines of your home. You only allow it to get out when seeking help from a trusted professional or from your pastor.

When Roles Are Not Defined

The next common cause of marital tension is role expectation. Roles ought to be clearly defined in the marriage so as to avoid conflicts and misunderstandings. *Who does what in the marriage must be clearly defined.* If roles are not clearly defined, a woman for instance will be left with all household chores she will feel enslaved. A wife must not be left to be the one who does gardening, laundry, cleans the house, cooks, washes the dishes, lays the bed, vacuums, mows the lawn, pays the bills and so forth whilst the man does nothing but watch television, eat and demand sex. That's being insensitive and uncaring.

If she works full time like the man and gets tired like he does, it will be barbaric and mischievous to leave all these chores to her. She must be helped out. To avoid misunderstandings and problems at home, roles ought to be clearly defined and agreed upon. Where the two of you get along so well and enjoy doing things together, there is no need then for roles to be defined since you both chip in to get chores done together.

Whereas roles are becoming a problem, the two of you must sit down and define your roles so as to avoid conflicts. Who does gardening, laundry, cleans the house, cooks, washes the dishes, lays the bed, vacuums, mows the lawn, pays the bills and what bills and so forth must be clearly defined.

When Finances Are Mismanaged

Women want three kinds of security: emotional, family and financial. Financial insecurity causes lots of problems at home. When it comes to finances, a husband and his wife must be transparent with each other. Remember: the basics of family finance are budgeting, saving, investment and spending wisely.

The couple must live with a budget where they know what comes in and what goes out, eliminating what expenses they know are not necessary. Spending wisely and being economically prudent helps avoid financial pressure, which is a hostile force and impediment to the desire of a successful marriage.

When Sex is Withheld

One of the reasons for anger and bitterness in most marriages is because sex is withheld from a partner or it's been used as a weapon of punishment. As I stated earlier, most women tend to be guilty with this, and the husbands tend not to take it lightly because they perceive it as a rejection of their manhood.

When this happens the mood at home can be adversely affected, leading to strife and prolonged misunderstanding.

The absence of regular and frequent sex is not healthy for any couple. The idea of marriage is togetherness and bonding, and sex fulfills that idea. Both husband and wife must have the mindset of cooperation and humility, where they willingly offer themselves in an exciting and involving manner to each other.

When There Is A Breakdown of Communication

It is necessary for a husband and wife to learn how to effectively communicate with each other. Communication is the process by which information is exchanged. Communication becomes effective when the husband understands the information his wife gives, and the wife understands the information her husband gives. Every marriage where the couples communicate respectfully and understandably will succeed. However, in the marriage where there is disrespect between husband and wife and an eventual breakdown of communication, the potential for marital disaster tends to be high.

One of the ways to overcome communication breakdown or the widening of the communication gap is by learning to be an effective communicator and listener. *You should be able to articulate your thoughts and feeling with love and reverence.* And when communicating, ensure you maintain eye contact with your spouse whilst you speak in the most civil of all tones.

Also, when your spouse is speaking to you, no matter what you're doing, you must stop, give him or her eye contact and pay attention to what he or she is saying. Even if you feel you already know what he or she is about to say and what he or she is about to say is fallacious, still give him or her eye contact and pay close attention.

Giving eye contact and paying close attention communicates to your husband or wife that he or she matters to you and what he or she is about to say is extremely important to you. This is one way of showing care and of avoiding marital tension.

When There Is Bitterness

The lack of power to excuse a spouse of their offenses can in the long run wreck a marriage. One of the characteristics of love is that it is forgiving and keeps no record of wrong. *No matter what your spouse might have done to upset you, you must be a Christian enough to forgive him or her.* Whether hurtful words spoken to you like an insult, a hurtful action like being smacked, or a hurtful behavior like ridiculing you before peers, have a forgiving heart.

When you fail to forgive, it will lead to bitterness and resentment and when you become bitter in your marriage, you open yourself up for the blockage of God's blessings in your life. In Colossians 3:19, couples are admonished to love each other without being bitter against themselves. As Christians, we are called upon to:

- Live lives that does not offend others, and

- Lives that are not offended by others

God doesn't want you to offend others and He as well does not want you to be offended by others. So in Philippians 1:10, we're admonished to live "without offense." Living with offense on the other hand means to refuse to forgive and to hold on to a hurt. *Refusing to forgive, especially your spouse places you in an awkward position where you stand to forfeit God's forgiveness.*

Remember in the Lord's Prayer, Jesus said in Matthew 6:14-15, "14 for if you forgive men their trespasses, your heavenly Father will also forgive you.   15 But if you do not forgive men their trespasses, neither will your Father forgive your trespasses." It is important that you live a life without offense. *If you harbor offense in your heart, you will lose the power to forgive the one who offended you, and when you fail to forgive, you are forfeiting the chance to experience God's forgiveness in return.* Since so much is at stake, I encourage you to live in harmony and walk in love toward your lover.

When There Is A Cultural Difference

Another common cause of marital tension is when there are cultural differences and the couple is not willing to adapt and adjust. Obviously, when two individuals grow in separate homes, with different upbringings, diverse background and dissimilar philosophies, the tendency for conflict is certainly very high. What the couple needs to do is to try and accept each other just the way they are without trying to do the impossible - change each other.

In accepting each other just the way you are, you must make some adjustments such as appreciating your distinguishable differences.

<u>When There Is Broken Trust</u>

One of the foundational stones on which to build a solid marriage is trust. If a husband and a wife desire a blissful marriage, they must trust each other totally and implicitly. *Nothing is able to damage a marriage as broken trust. When trust is broken, suspicion is aroused and when suspicion is aroused, nothing you do will please and satisfy your spouse.* That is why every couple must be honest to each other and live with integrity.

We live in a world where people are so insincere and dishonest it spills over to every area of their relationships including even their marriages. Husbands and wives playing secretive games with each other…"I can trust you with my body but I can't trust you with my phone and laptop" are common signal couples send to each other. So when a husband or wife is not by his or her phone for instance and the phone rings, he or she will scream; "don't answer it. I'll get it!" So a husband doesn't know the password to his wife's phone and email account and vice versa.

I once heard a preacher say that, because of insincerity and infidelity in marriages and because husbands and wives don't want each other to answer their phones, even when they go to the bathroom, they keep their phone in their hand as though it were a bar of soap.

In our marriage, we keep no secretive passwords. I know the passwords and pin numbers to all of my wife's accounts and gadgets and so does she. We use mobile me, so we share the contacts on our phones, so all the contacts on my phone is automatically synchronized with her phone and vice versa.

I am proposing for every husband and wife to be sincere with each other. I am proposing for every couple to share their passwords and pin numbers. Remember: if you fail to do so, you will be sowing seeds of distrust, which the enemy could use against your marriage in the long run. Be truthful. Be transparent. Be honest. Be trustworthy. Be a person of integrity. Integrity is being sincere with yourself, and honesty is being sincere with other people."

Let these two: integrity and honesty be your way of life.

When A Spouse Is Quick Tempered

Problems unfold in a marriage when a spouse does not tame his or her temper. If you make yourself better, things around you will become better. *If you want your spouse to be better in some area of character, make yourself better first, and your spouse will be better.* In order for a marriage to be successful, both husband and wife must be willing to change.

128

This desire for change become urgent when there is the problem of quick temper and sudden outburst of anger.

Anger is a state of being angry or a strong feeling or emotion that is oriented toward some real or supposed grievance.

What To Know About Anger

(I) Anger Is A Natural Emotion

It is okay to be angry but it is not all right to let your anger make you sin. Ephesians 4:26 says; "Be angry, and do not sin." Is this the Bible giving us counsel to be angry? Yes it is. It's okay to be angry as long as you don't sin. Example: when Jesus went to the temple and overturned the table of the traders. He showed an angry emotion, and the type of anger He displayed was not sinful because it was holy anger.

(II) Anger Can And Cannot Be Sinful

Anger is sinful when it is a negative emotion, and it becomes a negative emotion and sinful when it is:

(a) Causeless

This is when the person is angry for no reason or when the person displaces their anger on someone. Anger displacement occurs when the person is angered, let's say at work, but returns home with that fury and unconsciously displaces his or her anger and frustration on his or her spouse. Such outburst of negative emotion is causeless and sinful. The prudent thing to do is when you are ticked off at the office, you ensure you leave that negative emotion in the office building before you walk out of the door. Never carry the excess of a negative feeling from work to your home. Your home must be a place of love, peace and joy.

(b) Excessive

Furthermore, anger is sinful when it is excessive. Remember: Ephesians 4:29 wants you to be angry except that you should not let the anger make you sin. So showing an angry emotion is natural but it's unacceptable when such angry emotion is excessive. There are some people that once angered, are willing to cuss, curse, shove, hit and throw objects. This is what excessive anger is, and you must avoid that. If you're a man or woman whose anger is excessive, it will be difficult if not impossible to keep a happy home.

(c) Protracted

Lastly, anger is sinful when it is protracted or prolonged. Once again, let me remind you that although anger is a natural emotion, it is not okay to protract your anger. You will cause problems and tension in your marriage when you can get angry and hold on to your anger, going days without talking to your spouse.

The person who is quick tempered, gets angry causelessly, excessively, and protracts the anger is seen as unwise and not worthy of marriage. Ecclesiastes 7:9 reveals,

"...anger rests in the bosom of fools." God sees as a fool, the person who is quick tempered and manifests the above traits. Also Proverbs 22:24 says,

> *Make no friendship with an angry man, and with a furious man do not go.*

Do you see that? Make no friendship with an angry man! If the Lord doesn't want you to be the friend of an angry person or if you will, a quick tempered person, then, He implies we must not marry a person who is quick tempered and manifests the traits of causeless anger, excessive anger and protracted anger. If you fall within these categories, you must deliberately work your way out of this pit.

Marriage is for matured people and as you know, matured people master their emotions whereas immature people let their emotions master them.

How To Manage/Control Your Anger

> *So then, my beloved brethren, let every man be swift to hear, slow to speak, slow to wrath.*

> *James 1:19-20*

To manage your anger:

(1) Talk Less, Listen More

To manage your anger, you must talk less and listen more. In doing so, you must govern your emotions with wisdom and grace, and not with tantrums. Children throw tantrums because they are not matured, but since marriage is for matured people, throwing tantrums like a child is not the way to solving problems.

- Matured people don't throw tantrums, they act with wisdom and grace

- Simply tame your tongue when you feel angry

(2) Understand Your Anger

Ask yourself, "why am I angry?" "Do I get that angry at my computer when I need it to run faster but it tends to run slower?" "Is this anger a natural emotion or a negative one?"

- If it's a negative one, it's then sinful to harbor that emotional feeling in your heart.

- Ask God to forgive you and take the weight of that anger from your heart.

(3) Determine Your Anger Level

You should be able to tell if your anger is causeless, excessive or protracted. Try to ascertain the level of your anger. Are you just angry, bitter, annoyed, frustrated, deceived, disappointed, or mad?

- If you're feeling all of the above concurrently, it means your anger level is on the high side, and when you notice that you're extremely angry, that is when you must calm down.

- Your conscience or inner man will bear witness with the Holy Spirit that you're allowing the sun to go down on your anger. Immediately you receive this prompting, you must stop everything and ask the Holy Spirit to breath a fresh breathe of calm over you and walk away.

(4) Examine Your Anger Patterns

- Do you express anger in a way that overwhelms you and others?

- Do you get angrier than most people you know?

- Do you get angrier than is necessary?

- Do you use threatening language when angry?

(5) Think In Terms Of God's Word

Ask, what would Jesus do in a situation as this? What does God's Word say about the situation? If you think in line with God's Word, you would overcome anger.

- Aim for constructive expressions of your anger

- Think carefully before you say anything so you don't say something you regret

- Children and immature people talk before they think

- Matured folks think before they talk

(6) Purpose To Tame Your Temper

- Take time out (leave the situation)

- Do something physically asserting: run, jog or take a walk to unwind

- Practice deep breathing or repeat a calming word or phrase to yourself. Example: "I need to take it easy." "I need to calm down now." "It's wrong to be that mad at the love of my life. God forgive me."

There is no conflict that is beyond the realm of solvability. Every conflict is solvable when you make the Word of God your final authority to resolving differences. For all ten common causes of marital tension that we've discussed, including the uncommon ones, the Word of God has a solution for all those conflicts and therefore, don't underestimate what the life-changing Word of God is able to do with regards to providing you with wisdom and guidance to avoiding and overcoming the clashes and disagreements that come up in your marriage.

If you'll submit yourself to the authority of His Word and seek counsel and guidance from the Scriptures, no conflict whatsoever will be able to wreck your marriage.

Chapter 14

Tips To Enjoying Your Marriage

(1) Keep God In The Marriage

*Y*ou cannot prevent the creator and manufacturer of a product from being involved with his creation or production and hope to achieve maximum satisfaction using his product. Similarly, as the creator of marriage, you cannot keep God from being involved with His creation (in this case, your marriage) and hope to have a fulfilling and satisfactory marriage.

If you want your marriage to be blissful, keep God in the marriage. Pray for your spouse, your children, and your marriage and see if your love for each other will not grow from strength to strength.

135

Keep God in the marriage in four major ways:

I.   Pray together

There is a popular saying that a family that prays together sticks together. I fully subscribe to this truth. Every couple that wants to get God involved in their marriage must cultivate the discipline of praying together often. If possible pray together before and after bedtime.

II.   Study the Word of God together

Read the Bible to each other, memorize the Scriptures together and discuss what you read from the Word as a couple. The bottom-line is, you must have at least three times a week of family devotion and consecration.

III.   Be active in church

Every serious minded Christian couple doesn't just go to church. They are committed to their church and serve the church with their time, talents and treasures. Both husband and wife must serve in some ministry and in some capacity in the church primarily to ensure they are surrounded with Christian influence and people of likeminded faith.

In addition, going to church must be part of a couple's weekly activities. It's not enough to go to church and to register your name at the church. You must be involved, must wholeheartedly receive the Word that is taught and tailor your life, marriage and family with it.

(2) Easily Forgive

Never use hurtful or harsh words towards your spouse. Never insult or use demeaning behavior such as ridiculing your spouse in the presence of others. When offended, easily forgive. Bitterness and an unforgiving spirit cause marital tension and it can permanently drive your spouse away from you. *God forgave us of our sins, and He continues to forgive us when we sin. We also have to forgive others especially our spouses for their wrongdoings.*

(3) Love Yourselves

Express your love in all ways to your spouse. By all means search for his or her romance language and express love to him or her using the romance languages I taught earlier on. Relate to your spouse as your best friend. Have the welfare and wellbeing of your spouse at heart. Do romantic things for your spouse. Look romantic; be attractive; make your spouse want to have you all the time. Love yourselves sacrificially.

(4) Have Frequent Sex

Be intimate as often as possible. Never withhold yourself from your spouse. Lot's of sex between couple is great for the steadiness and stability of the marriage.

(5) Treat Yourselves As Partners

God created both the husband and the wife as coequals. Seek your spouse's opinion in decision-making and respect his or her views. You are partners not enemies so work as a team. Do your best to avoid quarrels and misunderstandings and seek to establish peace in the home. Your marriage is how you make it so give out your best without giving up. Speak to each other well. Your words must by all means be seasoned with grace and love.

You are partners and no one should be treated as though he or she were inferior. There is nowhere in the Bible where a husband or wife is to be treated as though he or she were subservient, subjugated or dealt with as though he or she were a slave or a servant.

When God formed Eve, He took one of Adam's ribs from his side to form her to indicate that the woman was not taken from under the man's foot but from his side to stand by him as his partner, associate and coequal.

(6) Be Committed

Be committed to your marriage. Divorce is never an option so make up your mind that you're marrying until death separates you. Marriage is for life so commit to love your spouse no matter what. Commit to do what your spouse asks you to do and seek to please him or her. Respect each other and treat each other with utmost admiration and dignity. After all, you're lovers, not enemies.

(7) Covenant Marriage

Remember: marriage is a covenant. Our God never breaks covenants. We've been created in His image, which means we must function like Him. Therefore, never break your marriage covenant. Marriage is supposed to mirror God's marriage to Israel and Christ's marriage to the church. God's marriage to Israel and Christ's marriage to the church is for the primary purpose of steadiness and permanence. Marriage must be for the same primary purpose and that is for permanence and as long as you both shall live. Marriage is God's creation, not man's idea and because it is God's intention, it's of a divine origin and not of a human origin. No human should try to annul what God has instituted. Thus, see your relationship with your spouse as a covenant relationship, which cannot be broken.

(8) Do What Is Expected Of You Well

One common reason for marital tension is role expectation. Role expectation has to do with "who does what" in the marriage. Who is responsible for what? Roles have to be clearly defined. "Who does what" has to be clearly defined. Basic roles such as who pays for what; who buys what; who cleans what; how do we manage our finances and so forth must be clearly defined.

God intended for marriage to be beautiful, blissful and a blessing. With this information at your fingertips, no man should be a liability to his wife, and no woman should be a burden to her husband. After reading this book, you should be well vested to be an asset and not a liability, a benefit and not a burden, a blessing and not a curse to your spouse.

God bless you and I pray for you that your marriage will

139

sizzle and be all that God intended for it to be. Fight for your marriage and no matter what work your marriage to work.

Another Great Book

By Sadick Arthur

DR. SADICK ARTHUR

THE

EFFECTIVE

LEADER

Qualities of Effective Leadership

Another Great Book

By Sadick Arthur

33 Guys & Girls YOU MUST NEVER MARRY

SADICK ARTHUR

Another Great Book

By Sadick Arthur

SADICK ARTHUR

DARE TO BE A DREAMER

HOW TO TURN YOUR DREAMS TO REALITY

Another Great Book

By Sadick Arthur

SADICK ARTHUR

GOD'S

PLAN FOR YOUR

FINANCIAL
SUCCESS

REALIZING YOUR FINANCIAL DESTINY